a Lukan Book of hours

BASIC FORMS OF THE DAILY OFFICE
OF THE ORDER OF SAINT LUKE

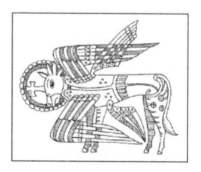

by Brothers and Sisters of the Order
Dwight W. Vogel, OSL, Editor and Compiler
Daniel T. Benedict, OSL, Abbot

2015

A Lukan Book of Hours:

Basic Forms of the Daily Office of The Order of Saint Luke

ISBN 978-1508553014

Editorial Consultants
Abbot Daniel Benedict, OSL,
Fran Ballinger, OSL, Jeanette Block, OSL,
Robert Davis, OSL, Jack Fahey, OSL,
Heather Josselyn-Cranson, OSL,
Elizabeth Moore, OSL

Elizabeth Moore, OSL, Production Editor

Commended by the Council of the General Chapter of The
Order of Saint Luke, May 21, 2015

This illustration of Saint Luke as an ox is public domain artwork found in *Fictitious and Symbolic Creatures in Art*, by John Vinycomb, [1909], page 55. The book can be found at sacred-texts.com.

The Winged Ox, Celtic artwork licensed to the Order of Saint Luke.

Starting in the lower left quadrant and moving counter-clockwise, the figures stand for the four gospel writers: Matthew, Mark, Luke and John. This and other images can be found at http://www.lanikennefick.com/animal-r-us/

Contents:

preface

Discovering the daily office as the prayer of the church has become a significant part of my spiritual journey. The "daily devotions," grace before meals, and "family altar" that were part of my childhood and youth were strong foundations, but the rich treasury of the historic practice of the Church in daily prayer has been an epiphany of grace for me.

In 1988, Abbot Michael J. O'Donnell of The Order of Saint Luke extended the call to service for me to prepare resources for praying the daily office in the context of the church year. Since that time the daily office has been an important part of both my scholarly work and my spiritual life. Three slim proto-type volumes, and then five volumes related to the seasons of the Christian calendar, including the text of hymns and psalms, resulted. Borrowing a phrase from Isaac Watts, that work was and continues to be both duty and delight for me.

Soon after his investiture, Abbot Daniel T. Benedict, OSL, asked me to respond to the call to service by preparing a new *Book of Offices and Services* and a one volume daily office. He appointed a Daily Office Revision Team and together we have worked on developing these resources for the Order and the wider church.

Time and experience has continued to teach those of us in the Order through the daily office as a school of prayer. While the offices contained in the *Book of Offices and Services* serve us well in such corporate settings as chapter and general chapter meetings and retreats, we came to recognize that they seemed to some to be unduly cumbersome for use in a solitary office (when prayed alone) or in the domestic church (when prayed with one's partner, family, or small group). Some of our members want and need the more fulsome, amplified form of the office; others desire a simpler, more basic form of the office. The Daily Office Revision Team set about developing both basic forms (which could be enriched) and amplified forms (which could be simplified) in our attempt to meet the needs of as many of our members as possible.

Then came one of those surprises of the Spirit: when provided with both an amplified form and a basic form, it was the simpler basic form that some of us found ourselves praying most often. We were praying it more faithfully. It fit into the pattern of our living so we were not as tempted to let it go under pressures of time and responsibility. It was a discipline we could keep more of the time. When basic forms for all the seasons but one had been developed, Abbot Daniel discerned that we needed to move ahead and provide a publication containing these basic forms so that others could share the experience we were having. The result is *A Lukan Book of Hours: Basic Forms of the Daily Office.* We are still at work preparing the amplified forms. They will have their time and place, and support the spiritual journey of some of our members most of the time and all of us from time to time, especially when we meet together.

For the work of the members of the team who have served as editorial consultants for this volume, I am deeply grateful. In addition to them, some of the many brothers and sisters who have helped us deserve our special gratitude. The work of Br. Richard Miller, OSL, not only as proofreader but as liturgical and theological consultant, has been invaluable. The knowledge and spiritual insights of Sr. Cheryl Brown, Ph.D., OSL, a scholar of Biblical languages, has been immensely helpful. It was her assessment of the translation in *The Inclusive Bible* which was a key factor in our choosing it as our primary Biblical text, not only because it shares the Order's own commitment to inclusive language, but because of its faithfulness to the languages of the Biblical text and its gift for rendering them in English in meaningful and significant ways. Br. George Crisp, OSL, has reviewed and critiqued my work on canticles and psalms with care.

From his initial vision through discernment of the need for this volume, to his care and insight about overall design as well as specific details, Abbot Daniel has supported this project with prayer and labor and wisdom. His generous spirit and personification of a Lukan spirituality underlie all that we are doing. I am especially grateful to Sr. Elizabeth [Sue] Moore, OSL, who brings to her role of production editor not only her ongoing work as a member of the Daily Office Revision Team but her own deep wisdom in seeking to live out a Lukan spirituality.

We share our work with you in the name of the holy and blessed Trinity, with the prayer that the Holy Spirit will guide both our efforts and your use of these resources. "Unless the Lord builds the house, they labor in vain who build it" (Psalm 127:1).

Dwight W. Vogel, OSL
Canon of The Order of Saint Luke
Pilgrim Place, Claremont, California
Ash Wednesday, 2015

CONTRIBUTORS

AMS   Ann Marie Sullivan, OSL
BG-C   Betsy Galloway-Carew, OSL
CAB   Cheryl A. Brown, OSL
DTB   Daniel T. Benedict, OSL
HJC   Heather Josselyn-Cranson, OSL
MJOD   Michael J. O'Donnell, OSL
TAR   Thomas A. Rand, OSL
TBE   Taylor Burton Edwards, OSL
TJC   Timothy J. Crouch, OSL
DWV   Dwight W. Vogel, OSL
Donald F. Chatfield
Jim Cotter
George R. Crisp, OSL
Ruth Duck
Elise Eslinger, OSL
Jeremy Hall, OSB
Bob Hurd
Patricia J. Patterson
Elizabeth J. Smith

ACKNOWLEDGMENTS

Responsible efforts have been made to trace the owner(s) and/or administrator(s) of each copyright. We regret any omission and will, upon written notice, make the necessary correction(s) in subsequent printings.

BCP, *The Book of Common Prayer,* The Church Hymnal Corporation; see Church Publishing, Inc.

ELLC, English Language Liturgical Consultation, www.englishtexts.org

NRSV, *New Revised Standard Version of the Bible,* Division of Christian Education of the National Council of the Churches of Christ in the United States of America; publisher: Thomas Nelson, Inc., Nashville, TN, 37214

OSH, (OSH Psalter), The Order of Saint Helena, 3042 Eagle Drive, Augusta, GA 30906-3346. Used with permission.

TEV *Today's English Version of the Bible* from The American Bible Society, 1965 Broadway, New York, NY 100223

TIB *The Inclusive Bible* by Priests for Equality; Sheed and Ward (imprint of Rowman & Littlefield Publishers, Inc.), 4501 Forbes Blvd., Suite 200, Lanham, MD 20706. Used with permission.
> Note: In keeping with *The Inclusive Psalter* published by Priests for Equality in 1997, ADONAI replaces YHWH in our use of texts from *The Inclusive Bible* © 2007.

Cairns Publications (Jim Cotter), administered by Canterbury Press (rights@hymnsam.org.uk)

Church Publishing Inc. 445 5th Ave., New York, NY 10016

Concordia Publishing House, 3558 South Jefferson Ave., St. Louis, MO 63118-3968; www.cph.org

UMH, *United Methodist Hymnal* , United Methodist Publishing House, Nashville TN

introduction

PRAYING THE HOURS OF THE DAILY OFFICE

In a Lukan understanding of daily prayer, grace, community, and discipleship converge. God's abounding grace comes to us in many ways. Among them is a means of grace we call the daily office. God's *grace* is already at work in us before we begin to pray--prompting us, inviting us, luring us to become aware of God's presence within and around us through times established for prayer. Known as the liturgy of the hours, some of these times date from the life of the early church.

The seven "hours" (offices or services) provided by The Order of Saint Luke follow the pattern of the seven hours listed by Basil the Great in the fourth century. There are two principal hours (Morning Prayer and Evening Prayer), three diurnal or daytime hours (mid-morning, mid-day, and mid-afternoon), and two nocturnal or nighttime hours (compline and vigil). These times of prayer recall the words of Psalm 119:164 -- "seven times a day I will praise you."

Many Christians engage in some form of personal or family "devotions." What is distinctive about praying the hours of the Daily Office? An office is a work done on behalf of others. In praying the Daily Office, we are called to recognize the sustaining *community* of the Holy Spirit of which we are a part, for we never pray apart from that community even when we are alone. Around the world and throughout the ages, we join with other members of the community of faith in the Church's prayer, praying on their behalf and joining in their prayer on behalf of others and the whole web of life. As we pray, God's grace strengthens, nourishes, forms, comforts, and delights us, sending us forth as part of God's kin-dom to embody God's healing grace for all creation.

1

An office is not only a work done on behalf of others, it entails certain responsibilities and duties. We are *disciples*, a word with the same root as the word discipline. All Christians are called to a life of prayer. Some Christians are called to the discipline of a daily pattern of prayer called "The Daily Office" with certain hours and shapes of prayer.

The Daily Office is also known as the liturgy of the hours. An hour, in addition to its reference to a sixty minute unit, is also a period of time in which something happens. We speak of "the hour of our death" or "our darkest hour", or a particular time of the day such as "the noon hour" or "the twilight hour". In this *Lukan Book of Hours,* the hours signify the times of day set apart for daily liturgical devotion.

We are not restricted to only one "right" way of doing this. God's grace is manifested to us in diverse ways. We are part of a community of diverse people with diverse needs and varieties of gifts. Stories in the gospels make clear that Jesus' call to discipleship means different things for different people. So it is, we believe, with hours of the Daily Office. As an Order, we are called to embody our discipleship of prayer through the Daily Office. However, we have differing needs, differing patterns of life, differing contexts, differing ways of sensing the Spirit. There are different seasons of the Spirit, and we do not all live in the same season at the same time, nor do many of us live in the same season of the Spirit throughout our life.

In this book, we provide basic forms for the liturgy of the hours. Our hope is that it will serve as a resource for those who feel called to, or are constrained by circumstances to:
- pray a brief, relatively simple office;
- pray a stable office with the same basic content throughout a season; and
- pray with fewer words and greater opportunities for extended silence.

These services embody the depth dynamic that underlies the historic Daily Office: an opening rite, psalter and gloria, scripture and canticle, prayers, and going forth.

The hours of the Daily Office have their own distinctive nature; they do not replicate services of Word and Table. Like them, the hours of the daily office draw us into the paschal mystery, but as reflected in the pattern of daily life and the play of light and dark—quite literally the liturgy of the hours! Whether the service of the hour is long or short, basic or amplified, it embodies a celebration of God's *grace* in the paschal mystery, a sense of being in *community* with our brothers and sisters, and a way of living out our *discipleship* in the cycles of time in terms of the hours of the day, the seasons of the liturgical and solar year, and the unfolding mystery of Christ and cosmos.

DIRECTIONS FOR PRAYING THE MORNING AND EVENING HOURS

If you want or need *a simple, brief, basic service:*
- Use the service just as it appears without turning to any other resource. That will provide you with several stanzas of hymns, a heartword from a psalm and a heartword from scripture, brief prayers and space for your own prayers. Heartwords are passages of scripture that should take residence in our hearts, speaking to us and for us, forming us as God's beloved community.
- By honoring the suggested times of silence, this approach can help us avoid being bogged down by too many words.

If you want or need a service that is *somewhat fuller in nature*, but doesn't involve using another book:

- Include a psalm from later in the book. The psalms included can change day by day.
- Include a canticle from later in the book. The canticles change season by season.
- Using one or both of these options will ground the service more fully in scriptures that provide the bedrock for our spirituality.

Finally, there are at least three points at which you may choose to use resources beyond this volume:
- Additional psalms as indicated in a psalm lectionary, or by reading through the psalter psalm by psalm.
- Scripture readings for the day designated in a daily lectionary, or a *lectio continua* (continual reading from a book of the Bible) of your own choosing.
- A reading for meditation and reflection from a source of your choosing.
- Using any or all of these provides *a more fulsome approach* to praying the hour.

What one needs or is called or constrained to do in praying the Daily Office may change from morning to night, from day to day, from season to season, from year to year. Be attentive to the promptings of the Spirit, and be open to God's calls to the discipleship of prayer which may (and likely will) change. In all this, God's grace is at work--calling us, challenging us, forming us into a community of prayer. To that end, we offer to God and to you these basic forms of praying the Daily Office with the prayer that the Holy Spirit will use them and us in the service of Christ's kin-dom.

HOW WE TALK TO AND ABOUT GOD: OUR USE OF ADONAI AND Adonai

People call me by several names. Some are more formal ("Dr., Pastor, Professor Vogel"). Some imply friendship or relationship ("Br. Dwight" or just plain "Dwight"—although in our culture a first name has become a preferred form of address even by those who know nothing more about me than my name—but I hope it implies the hope to know me better!). But there are also the "secret names" used only by my beloved, implying a deep personal relationship, and evoking a sense of covenant bond. Something like that is at stake in the names the Biblical writers use in talking to and about God.

Whenever ADONAI (all upper case letters) occurs in this book, it represents YHWH in the Hebrew text (See Exodus 3:14). YHWH is the sacred, covenant name of God, often designated as "the tetragrammaton" ("four letters"). YHWH carries the rich meaning of One whose "is-ness" in the past, the present and the future is actively and passionately present for us and all creation; it evokes a sense of both transcendence and personal relationship.

Early in post-exilic Judaism, YHWH was deemed too sacred to pronounce, so it was written in the Hebrew text without vowels. However, because Jews needed to pronounce the word in order to read it aloud in Temple and Synagogue, they began to substitute *adonai*, a Hebrew term of reverence, honor and respect, denoting—most frequently—Lord, Master, Sovereign.

In the 3rd century BCE, those who translated the Hebrew text into Greek rendered YHWH as *kurios*, which corresponds in meaning to *adonai* (and cognate forms) in Hebrew. Likewise, in Jerome's translation of the Latin Vulgate (4th c. ce), he translated YHWH by forms of *dominus* (Lord, Master, Sovereign). These Greek and Latin renderings stand behind many contemporary English translations of YHWH in the Hebrew Bible. In them, YHWH appears as LORD (uppercase

5

letters); and references to God as *adonai* (or cognate forms) in the Hebrew text appear as "Lord" (lower case letters).

We have chosen to render YHWH as ADONAI rather than LORD, because in contemporary English usage, the word LORD carries cultural baggage from feudal times that could cause us to understand the divine name incorrectly, even negatively (as sexist or imperialist), and to miss the rich meaning of YHWH as the covenant name of the God of Israel. Likewise, in response to the call for inter-religious understanding and sensitivity inherent in a Lukan spirituality, we wish to identify with our Jewish brothers and sisters, who pronounce YHWH as ADONAI. When *Adonai* (or cognate forms) occurs in the Hebrew text in reference to God, and sometimes when *kurios* occurs in the Greek, we render it in English as "Adonai," in order to avoid the same problems with possible misinterpretation due to contemporary understandings of words like "Lord." As it was for the early church, the referent is often ambiguous, pointing to either (or both) God and Christ. It was partly out of the experience of such language that the Church's understanding of Christology and of "the holy and blessed Trinity" emerged.

Thus, as we use ADONAI here, our limited language seeks to evoke a sense of both transcendence and personal relationship, pointing to One whose "is-ness" is actively and passionately present for us and all creation, as well as One to whom we owe allegiance as we respond to the invitation: "Come, follow me."

Br. Dwight Vogel, OSL

CHANTING THE PSALM TONES
See p. 133.

See p. 133.

Augustine observes that those who sing pray twice. Chanting psalms and canticles gives wings of song to our prayers. The following practices encourage that to happen:
- Psalm tones are to be sung quietly with a meditative spirit, even when they are acts of praise.
- Punctuation (such as a comma or semicolon) should usually be observed with a short break.
- Psalm tones are not be hurried; take time to breathe as indicated below.

When singing a psalm tone:
- If there is accompaniment, let the initial chord sound first as you take a short breath;
  then begin singing.
- The **first note** is a reciting note to which one or more syllables or words are sung.
- A slightly indented line indicates the reciting note is continuing on it.
- On the underlined syllable(s), move to the **first black note**.
- Sing the syllable(s) before the italicized syllable(s) on the **second black note**.
- Sing the **italicized syllable(s)** to the half note before the bar line.
- In the text, an **asterisk (*)** indicates where that median bar line comes. Take a short breath before continuing.
- Follow the same directions for the second half of the psalm tone.
  At the end of the psalm tone, take a breath before continuing.

Example:

PSALM TONE ONE

(short breath when beginning)
I will sing praises <u>to</u> your *name.* * *(short breath)*
You are the stronghold of my life; *(brief break)*
You are the Rock of <u>my</u> sal-*vation. (breath)*

Note: In the antiphons for the psalms, the text for the antiphon is printed in italics while the syllable(s) sung to the last note are not italicized: *I will sing praises <u>to</u> your* name.

morning and evening hours of prayer

to be surrounded and infused
with moments of silence
and listening

morning prayer
throughout advent

OPENING

SMALL CAPS: CALL TO PRAISE AND PRAYER AND REMEMBRANCE OF BAPTISM

O God, open our lips,
and our mouths shall proclaim your praise.
By Word and water God renews us this day
in the living fountain of God's grace
**and raises us with Christ Jesus to live
a new life in the Spirit.**
Remember your baptism and be thankful!
(water may be touched or poured)

MORNING HYMN   88.88 LM

Tune: VENI EMMANUEL (*UMH* 211)

O come, O Dayspring, come and cheer
our spirits by your advent here.
Disperse the gloomy clouds of night,
and death's dark shadows put to flight.
Rejoice! Rejoice!
Emmanuel is coming near;
let Love dispel all fear.

Henry Sloan Coffin, 1916, adapted from John Mason Neale, 1851 (alt.)
Refrain: Eva Fleishner, 2008

MORNING PRAYER

O Word fulfilling every word,
O God incarnate in our flesh!
Emmanuel! Expected One!
God-with-us now in Bread till time is done!
O God of all our longing,
be all things to us now and to eternity! **Amen.**

Adapted from Meditations on the O Antiphons (Jeremy Hall, OSB)

PSALTER

PSALM

O Mighty God of Hosts, re-turn to us--- *
let your face smile on us and we will be *saved!*

Psalm 80:19 TIB

(See pp. 90-98 or a psalm lectionary for additional psalter readings)

Glory to you, O Trinity, most holy and *blessed;* *
One God, now and for-ever. A-*men.*

SILENCE

WORD

[CANTICLE *(see p. 116)*]

SCRIPTURE

(see daily lectionary for additional appropriate readings, or)
Prepare the way of the Lord,
make straight in the desert a highway for our God.

Adapted from Isaiah 40:3

SILENCE

AN EXCERPT FROM THE CANTICLE OF ZECHARIAH

(See p. 112 for complete form)

(may be chanted to Psalm Tone 3)

We bless you, Adonai, God of *Israel,* *
for you come to visit us
   and ransom us from *bondage.*
You have brought forth a strong De-*liverer**
in the house of your child, *David.*
Through your merciful compassions, God our *God,* *
the dawn from on high shall *visit us,*
to shine on those kept in dungeons
   and the shadows of *death**
and to guide our feet into the paths of *peace.*

TBE

11

PRAYERS

Give thanks and pray for the coming day and the needs of the world.
    (See p. 131)
[Prayers of special intention such as prayers for a holy day or the
Collect for the Order (see pp. 128-129) may be included.]

The Lord's Prayer   *(See pp. 126-127)*

Concluding Collect
    Come, O come Emmanuel:
    you are the way, the truth and the life;
    you are the true vine and the bread of life.
    Come, living Savior,
    come to your world which waits for you. **Amen**.

OSL

Hymn   76.76 D
                                         Tune: ELLACOMBE (*UMH* 203)
    Hail to the Lord's Anointed, great David's greater Son!
    Hail in the time appointed, his reign on earth begun!
    He comes to break oppression, to set the captive free;
    to take away transgression, and rule in equity.

James Montgomery, 1821

Going Forth
    May the God of hope
        fill us with all joy and peace in believing,
    so that, by the power of the Holy Spirit,
        we may abound in hope.

Adapted from Romans 15:13 *RSV*
    The grace of the Lord Jesus Christ be with us.
    Let us bless the Lord. **Thanks be to God**.

evening prayer
throughout advent

OPENING

ENTRANCE OF THE LIGHT

Jesus Christ, you are the light of the world,
the light no darkness can overcome.
Stay with us, for it is evening,
and the day is nearly over.

HYMN OF LIGHT

(may be sung to psalm tone 1; for complete form see p. 130)
O gra-cious *Light,* *
pure brightness of our everlasting God in *heaven,*
O Je-sus *Christ,* * ho-ly and *blessed.*
Now as we come to the setting of the *sun,* *
and our eyes behold the ves-per *light,*
we sing your praises, O *God,* *
most holy and bless-ed *Trinity.*

Excerpted from "Phos hilaron," late 3rd/early 4th c.;
adapted by Timothy J. Crouch , O.S.L.
from the work of Charles Mortimer Guilbert

PRAYER OF AWARENESS AND ASSURANCE

(a recollection of Christ present in the moments of the day)
Holy God, purify the secrets of our hearts and mercifully
forgive us that, being renewed and restored by the
benediction of your love, we may await the coming of
Jesus Christ as we pray: "Come, Lamb of God, and do
not let us hinder your coming." **Amen.**

Adapted from the Gallican Sacramentary 5th c.
and *Rorate caeli,* ancient Advent text

Silence

May God who said, "Let light shine out of darkness,"
shine in our hearts
to give us the light of the knowledge of the glory of God
in the face of Jesus Christ.

Adapted from II Corinthians 4:6 *NRSV*

We are a forgiven people! **Thanks be to God!**

PSALTER

Psalm

Let the nations shout and <u>sing</u> for *joy**
for you dispense true justice <u>to</u> the *world*.

Psalm 67:4a TIB

*(See pp. 100-107 or a psalm lectionary for additional
psalter readings)*

Glory to you, O Trinity, most <u>holy</u> and *blessed;**
One God, now and for-<u>ever</u>. A-*men*.

Silence

WORD

[Canticle *(See p. 116)*]

Scripture

(see daily lectionary for additional appropriate readings, or)
Make ready the way of our God;
clear a straight path.
The twisted paths will be made straight,
and the rough road smooth—
and all humankind will see the salvation of God.

Adapted from Luke 3:4-6 TIB

Silence

An Excerpt from the Canticle of Mary
(See p. 114 for complete form)
(may be chanted to psalm tone 2)
My soul proclaims your <u>great</u>-ness, *Lord;**
my spirit rejoices in <u>you</u>, my *Savior;*
You have mercy on <u>those</u> who *fear you**
in every <u>gen</u>-er-*ation*.
You have cast the mighty <u>from</u> their *thrones;**
you have lifted <u>up</u> the *lowly*.
You have filled the hungry <u>with</u> good *things;**
and the rich have been <u>sent a</u>-way *empty*.

You have come to the help of your ser-vant *Israel,* *
for you have remembered your promise of *mercy.*

TJC

[A READING FOR MEDITATION AND REFLECTION]

PRAYERS

Pray for the life of the church and the world and the concerns of the heart. (See p. 131)
[Prayers of special intention such as prayers for a holy day or the Collect for the Order (see pp. 128-129) may be included.]

THE LORD'S PRAYER *(See pp. 126-127)*

CONCLUDING COLLECT

Bridegroom of all things, creation waits for you.
As the sun sets, come among us in quiet hope,
and, on the morrow, come, be vigilant in us
to embody the compassion and justice of your reign.
Amen.

DTB

HYMN   87.87 D; Tune: HYFRYDOL (*UMH* 196)

Come, thou long-expected Jesus,
born to set thy people free;
from our fears and sins release us,
let us find our rest in thee.
Israel's strength and consolation,
hope of all the earth thou art;
dear desire of every nation,
joy of every longing heart.

Charles Wesley, 1744

GOING FORTH

May the God of peace preserve us whole and complete
—spirit, soul and body—
at the coming of our Savior Jesus Christ.

Adapted from I Thessalonians 5:23 *TIB*

The grace of the Lord Jesus Christ be with us.
Let us bless the Lord. **Thanks be to God.**

morning prayer
from christmas day through epiphany

OPENING

CALL TO PRAISE AND PRAYER AND REMEMBRANCE OF BAPTISM

O God, open our lips,
and our mouths shall proclaim your praise.
By Word and water God renews us this day
in the living fountain of God's grace
**and raises us with Christ Jesus to live
a new life in the Spirit.**
Remember your baptism and be thankful!
(water may be touched or poured)

MORNING HYMN   77.77 D
Tune: MENDELSSOHN, (*UMH* 240)

Hail the heaven-born Prince of Peace!
Hail the Sun of Righteousness!
Light and life to all he brings,
risen with healing in his wings.
Mild he lays his glory by,
born that we no more may die,
born to raise us from the earth,
born to give us second birth.
Hark! the herald angels sing,
"Glory to the newborn King!"

Charles Wesley, 1739; Alt.

MORNING PRAYER

Emmanuel, God-with-us,
shine the light of your coming in our hearts
and inflame them with your love,
that we may shine with Christ as blazing lights
giving praise for the mystery of your incarnation.
Amen.

Adapted from the Gelasian Sacramentary 5th c.

PSALTER

PSALM

Let the fields exult and all <u>that</u> is *in them.* *
Let all the trees of the forest sing for joy
for the <u>Savior</u> is *born!*

Adapted from Psalm 96:12 TIB

(See pp. 90-98 or a psalm lectionary for additional psalter readings)

Glory to you, O Trinity, most <u>holy</u> and *blessed;* *
One God, now and for-<u>ever</u>. A-*men*.

SILENCE

WORD

[CANTICLE *(See p. 117)*]

SCRIPTURE

(see daily lectionary for additional appropriate readings, or)
And the Word became flesh
and tabernacled among us;
and we have seen the Word's glory,
filled with grace, filled with truth.

Adapted from John 1:14, a-c, e-f, TIB

SILENCE

AN EXCERPT FROM THE CANTICLE OF ZECHARIAH
(See p. 112 for complete form)

(may be chanted to Psalm Tone 3)

We bless you, Adonai, <u>God</u> of *Israel,* *
for you come to visit us
and ransom <u>us</u> from *bondage.*
You have brought forth a <u>strong</u> De-*liverer* *
in the house of <u>your</u> child, *David.*
Through your merciful compassions, <u>God</u> our *God,* *
the dawn from on <u>high</u> shall *visit us,*
to shine on those kept in dungeons
and the <u>shadows</u> of *death* *
and to guide our feet into the <u>paths</u> of *peace.*

TBE

[A READING FOR MEDITATION AND REFLECTION]

PRAYERS

Give thanks and pray for the coming day and the needs of the world.
    (See p. 131)
[Prayers of special intention such as prayers for a holy day or the
    Collect for the Order (see pp. 128-129) may be included.]

THE LORD'S PRAYER   *(See pp. 126-127)*

CONCLUDING COLLECT
        Adonai, our Emmanuel,
        you are the way, the truth, and the life;
        you are the true vine and the bread of life.
        We rejoice that you have come
            to tabernacle among us.
        Be born anew in us today
        that, by your grace, we may follow you faithfully.
        Amen.

                                                            OSL

HYMN   Irr., Tune: CRANHAM (*UMH* 221)
        What can I give him,
        poor as I am?
        If I were a shepherd,
        I would bring a lamb;
        if I were a Wise Man,
        I would do my part;
        yet what I can I give him:
        give my heart.

                                        Christina G. Rossetti, 1872

GOING FORTH
        We have seen Christ's glory,
            glory as of God's Chosen One,
        full of grace, full of truth!

                                            Adapted from John 1:14

        The grace of the Lord Jesus Christ be with us.
        Let us bless the Lord. **Thanks be to God**.

evening prayer
from christmas day through epiphany

OPENING

ENTRANCE OF THE LIGHT

    Jesus Christ, you are the light of the world,
    the light no darkness can overcome.
    Stay with us, for it is evening,
    and the day is nearly over.

HYMN OF LIGHT

    (may be sung to psalm tone 1; for complete form see p. 130)
    O gra-cious *Light,* *
    pure brightness of our everlasting God in *heaven,*
    O Je-sus *Christ,* * ho-ly and *blessed.*
    Now as we come to the setting of the *sun,* *
    and our eyes behold the ves-per *light,*
    we sing your praises, O *God,* *
    most holy and bless-ed *Trinity.*

> Excerpted from "Phos hilaron," late 3rd/early 4th c.;
> adapted by Timothy J. Crouch , O.S.L.
> from the work of Charles Mortimer Guilbert

PRAYER OF AWARENESS AND ASSURANCE

  (a recollection of Christ present in the moments of the day)
    Faithful and loving God,
    we lift up our words and thoughts and deeds this day.
    Where we have gone astray, forgive us.
    Where we are unaware of the wrong we have done,
    sensitize us to your reign of peace and justice.
    Be born in us; abide with us.
    We trust in your forgiving grace and empowering love.

> DWV

Silence

    May God who said, "Let light shine out of darkness,"
      shine in our hearts

to give us the light of the knowledge of the glory of God
in the face of Jesus Christ.

Adapted from II Corinthians 4:6

We are a forgiven people! **Thanks be to God!**

PSALTER

PSALM

I will listen to what you have to say, _A_ –DO-_NAI_-- *
Your salvation is near to those <u>who</u> re-_vere you._
Love and faithful-<u>ness</u> have _met,_*
justice and peace <u>have</u> em-_braced._

Psalm 85:8a, 9a, 10 TIB

*(See pp. 100-107 or a psalm lectionary for additional psalter
readings)*

Glory to you, O Trinity, most <u>holy</u> and _blessed;_*
One God, now and for-<u>ever</u>. A-_men._

SILENCE

WORD

[CANTICLE *(See p. 117)*]

SCRIPTURE
(see daily lectionary for additional appropriate readings, or)
The people who walked in darkness
have seen a great light.
The light shines in the darkness,
and the darkness has not overcome it.

Adapted from Isaiah 9:2 and John 1:5

SILENCE

AN EXCERPT FROM THE CANTICLE OF MARY
(See p. 114 for complete form)
(may be chanted to psalm tone 2)
My soul proclaims your <u>great</u>-ness, _Lord;_*
my spirit rejoices in <u>you</u>, my _Savior;_

You have mercy on <u>those</u> who *fear you**
in every <u>gen</u>-er-*ation.*
You have cast the mighty <u>from</u> their *thrones;**
you have lifted <u>up</u> the *lowly.*
You have filled the hungry <u>with</u> good *things;**
and the rich have been <u>sent a</u>-way *empty.*
You have come to the help of your <u>ser</u>-vant *Israel,**
for you have remembered your <u>promise</u> of *mercy*

TJC

[A READING FOR MEDITATION AND REFLECTION]

PRAYERS

Pray for the life of the church and the world and the concerns of the heart. (See p. 131.)
[Prayers of special intention such as prayers for a holy day or the Collect for the Order (see pp. 128-129) may be included.]

THE LORD'S PRAYER   *(See pp. 126-127)*
CONCLUDING COLLECT
>God-with-us,
>may the deep wonder of Christmas joy
>   be ours this night;
>may the transforming presence of Christ's love
>   for this hurting world take shape within us;
>and may the healing power of Christ's grace
>   for all creation
>awaken in us even as we sleep.
>In the name of the Word made flesh we pray. **Amen.**

DWV

HYMN
87.87.887
Tune: DIVINUM MYSTERIUM
(BOS 112, UMH 184)

Of the Parent's heart begotten,
ere the worlds began to be,
he is Alpha and Omega,
he the source, the ending he

21

of the things that are, that have been,
and that future years shall see,
evermore and evermore!

Aurelius Clemens Prudentius (348-c. 410);
tr. John Mason Neale (1818-1866)

GOING FORTH

Send out your light and your truth, let them lead us.
With you is the fountain of light,
and in your light may we see light!

Adapted from Psalm 43:3 and 36:9

The grace of the Lord Jesus Christ be with us.
Let us bless the Lord. **Thanks be to God**.

.

morning prayer
for ordinary time after epiphany

OPENING

CALL TO PRAISE AND PRAYER AND REMEMBRANCE OF BAPTISM

O God, open our lips,
and our mouths shall proclaim your praise.
By Word and water God renews us this day
in the living fountain of God's grace
and raises us with Christ Jesus to live
a new life in the Spirit.
Remember your baptism and be thankful!
(water may be touched or poured)

MORNING HYMN   88.88 LM
Tune: GIFT OF LOVE (*UMH* 408)

A holy house has wisdom made,
with finest food her table laid.
Here shall the hungry have their fill.
Here shall the broken heart be healed.

Nourish us now, Incarnate One,
around the table of your love,
and grow the kin[g]dom in our midst
where righteousness and mercy kiss.

© 2014 Bob Hurd (used with permission)

MORNING PRAYER

Eternal God, fill the world with your glory,
and enable us to reflect the radiance of your light
in works of justice and compassion,
through Jesus Christ our Lord. **Amen.**

Adapted from traditional sources, OSL

PSALTER

PSALM

You see every trouble, every <u>cause</u> for *grief;**
you ponder it and take it <u>into</u> your *hand.*

ADONAI, you hear the desire of the *meek,* *
You strengthen their hearts and bend your ear to *them.*

Psalm 10:14b, 17 *TIB*

(See pp. 90-98 or a psalm lectionary for additional psalter readings)

Glory to you, O Trinity, most holy and *blessed;* *
One God, now and for-ever. A-*men.*

SILENCE

WORD

[CANTICLE *(See p. 118)*]

SCRIPTURE
(see daily lectionary for additional appropriate readings, or)
You are a chosen people, a royal priesthood, a
consecrated people set apart to sing the praises of the
One who called you out of darkness into the wonderful,
divine light.

Adapted from I Peter 2:9 *TIB*

SILENCE

AN EXCERPT FROM THE CANTICLE OF ZECHARIAH
(See 112 for complete form)
(may be chanted to Psalm Tone 3)
We bless you, Adonai, God of *Israel,* *
for you come to visit us
and ransom us from *bondage.*
You have brought forth a strong De-*liverer**
in the house of your child, *David.*
Through your merciful compassions, God our *God,* *
the dawn from on high shall *visit us,*
to shine on those kept in dungeons
and the shadows of *death**
and to guide our feet into the paths of *peace.*

TBE

[A READING FOR MEDITATION AND REFLECTION]

PRAYERS

Give thanks and pray for the coming day and the needs of the world.
(See p. 131)
[Prayers of special intention such as prayers for a holy day or the
Collect for the Order (see pp. 128-129) may be included.]

THE LORD'S PRAYER   *(See pp. 126-127)*

CONCLUDING COLLECT

God of love and justice:
Give us such an awareness of your mercies
that with truly thankful hearts
we may show forth your praise
not only with our lips but in our lives
by giving ourselves to your service
in the name of Jesus, our Emmanuel. **Amen.**

Adapted from BCP

HYMN   88.88 LM; Tune: DUKE STREET (*UMH* 438)

Forth in your name, O Lord, we go,
our daily labor to pursue;
You, only you, resolved to know,
in all we think or speak or do.

The task your wisdom has assigned,
O let us cheerfully fulfill,
in all our works your presence find,
and prove your good and perfect will.

Adapted from a hymn of Charles Wesley (1707-1788)

GOING FORTH

The God of all grace, who has called us to eternal glory
in Christ, establish and strengthen us by the power of
the Holy Spirit, that we may live in grace and peace.

Adapted from I Peter 5:10, OSL

The grace of the Lord Jesus Christ be with us.
Let us bless the Lord. **Thanks be to God.**

evening prayer
ordinary time after epiphany

OPENING

ENTRANCE OF THE LIGHT

> Jesus Christ, you are the light of the world,
> **the light no darkness can overcome.**
> Stay with us, for it is evening,
> **and the day is nearly over.**

HYMN OF LIGHT

> *(may be sung to psalm tone 1; for complete form see p. 130)*
> O gra-cious *Light,* *
> pure brightness of our everlasting God in *heaven,*
> O Je-sus *Christ,* * ho-ly and *blessed.*
> Now as we come to the setting of the *sun,* *
> and our eyes behold the ves-per *light,*
> we sing your praises, O *God,* *
> most holy and bless-ed *Trinity.*

Excerpted from "Phos hilaron," late 3rd/early 4th c.;
adapted by Timothy J. Crouch , O.S.L.

from the work of Charles Mortimer Guilbert

PRAYER OF AWARENESS AND ASSURANCE

> *(a recollection of Christ present in the moments of the day)*
> O God of ocean, raindrop and font,
> we see the tears of the world and turn away.
> We hoard our little cups of moisture,
> yet our hearts have dried out.
> Cleanse your people with your tears of love,
> and raise us up to live as a baptized people. **Amen**.

BG-C, alt.

Silence

> May God who said, "Let light shine out of darkness,"
> shine in our hearts
> to give us the light of the knowledge of the glory of God
> in the face of Jesus Christ.

Adapted from II Corinthians 4:6

> We are a forgiven people! **Thanks be to God!**

PSALTER

PSALM

I said, "Who will take my side against the corrupt?
  Who will stand by me a-<u>gainst</u> the *violent?"**
But ADONAI is my fortress;
  my God is my <u>Rock</u> of *Refuge.*

Psalm 94:16, 22 TIB

(See pp. 100-107 or a psalm lectionary for additional psalter readings)

Glory to you, O Trinity, most <u>holy</u> and *blessed;
One God, now and for-<u>ever</u>. A-*men.***

SILENCE

WORD

[CANTICLE *(See p. 118)*]

SCRIPTURE

(see daily lectionary for additional appropriate readings, or)
May the word of Christ dwell in you richly.
Whatever you do in word or deed,
do everything in the name of the Lord Jesus,
giving thanks to God.

Colossians 3:16a, 17 OSL

SILENCE

AN EXCERPT FROM THE CANTICLE OF MARY

(See p. 114 for complete form)
                    (may be chanted to psalm tone 2)
My soul proclaims your <u>great</u>-ness, *Lord;**
my spirit rejoices in <u>you</u>, my *Savior;*
You have mercy on <u>those</u> who *fear you**
in every <u>gen</u>-er-*ation.*
You have cast the mighty <u>from</u> their *thrones;**
you have lifted <u>up</u> the *lowly.*

You have filled the hungry <u>with</u> good *things;**
and the rich have been <u>sent a</u>-way *empty.*
You have come to the help of your <u>ser</u>-vant *Israel,**
for you have remembered your <u>promise</u> of *mercy.*

TJC

[A Reading for Meditation and Reflection]

PRAYERS

Pray for the life of the church and the world and the concerns of the heart. (See p. 131.)
[Prayers of special intention such as prayers for a holy day or the Collect for the Order (see pp. 128-129) may be included.]

THE LORD'S PRAYER   *(See pp. 126-127)*
CONCLUDING COLLECT
God ever with us,
we belong to you through the incarnation,
   death and resurrection of Christ Jesus.
May we live his dying and rising
   in compassion and risky vigilance,
seeing the poor and the oppressed
   as Jesus living among us
and keeping vigil for the coming of your reign
   of peace and justice. **Amen**.

DTB, alt.

HYMN   Irr. Tune: SOMOS DEL SEÑOR
                                        (*BOS* 52, *UMH* 356)
When we are living, it is in Christ Jesus,
and when we're dying it is in the Lord.
Both in our living and in our dying,
we belong to God, we belong to God.

To pain and sorrow, Christ brings shalom.
In peace and justice, Christ brings shalom.
So when we're living the way of Jesus,
we are God's shalom, we are God's shalom.

St. 1, anon (Romans 14:8-9)
translation and st. 2 Elise Eslinger, OSL

GOING FORTH

> May we be made strong with strength coming from
> God, and may we be prepared to endure everything
> with patience as we joyfully give thanks to the One who
> enables us to share in the inheritance of the saints in
> light.
>
> Adapted from Colossians 1:11-12 OSL

> The grace of the Lord Jesus Christ be with us.
> Let us bless the Lord. **Thanks be to God**.

mornịng prayer
for Lent

OPENING

CALL TO PRAISE AND PRAYER AND REMEMBRANCE OF BAPTISM

O God, open our lips,
and our mouths shall proclaim your praise.
By Word and water God renews us this day
in the living fountain of God's grace
and raises us with Christ Jesus to live
a new life in the Spirit.
Remember your baptism and be thankful!
(water may be touched or poured)

MORNING HYMN

88.88 LM
Tune: GERMANY ("Take up thy cross")
(*UMH* 415)

O love, how deep, how broad, how high,
it fills the heart with ecstasy,
that God, the son of God should take
our mortal form for mortals' sake.

For us baptized, for us he bore
the holy fast and hungered sore,
for us temptation sharp he knew;
for us the tempter overthrew.

Benjamin Webb, 1854 alt.

MORNING PRAYER

Write your blessed name, O Lord, upon our hearts,
there to remain so indelibly engraved
that no prosperity, no adversity
shall ever move us from your love.

Be to us a strong tower of defense,
a comforter in tribulation, a deliverer in distress,
a very present help in trouble,

and a guide to heaven
through the many temptations
and dangers of this life. **Amen.**

Thomas a Kempis 15th c. (alt.)

PSALTER

PSALM

I wait for you, O God; my soul waits for you;
   in your word is my *hope.* *
My soul waits for you,
   more than sentries for the *morning.*

Psalm 130:5-6 OSH

(See pp. 90-98 or a psalm lectionary for additional psalter readings)

Glory to you, O Trinity, most holy and *blessed;* *
One God, now and for-ever. A-*men*.

SILENCE

WORD

[CANTICLE *(see p. 119)*]

SCRIPTURE
   (see daily lectionary for additional appropriate readings, or)
   Let us lay aside every weight and sin
      that clings so closely,
   and let us run with perseverance the race
      that is set before us,
   looking to Jesus, the pioneer and perfecter of our faith.

Adapted from Hebrews 12:1-2 NRSV, OSL

SILENCE

AN EXCERPT FROM THE CANTICLE OF ZECHARIAH
   (See 112 for complete form)
                           (may be chanted to Psalm Tone 3)
   We bless you, Adonai, God of *Israel,* *
      for you come to visit us
      and ransom us from *bondage.*

You have brought forth a <u>strong</u> De-*liverer**
   in the house of <u>your</u> child, *David.*
Through your merciful compassions, <u>God</u> our *God,**
the dawn from on <u>high</u> shall *visit us,*
to shine on those kept in dungeons
   and the <u>shadows</u> of *death**
and to guide our feet into the <u>paths</u> of *peace.*

TBE

[A READING FOR MEDITATION AND REFLECTION]

PRAYERS

Give thanks and pray for the coming day and the needs of the world.
   (See p. 131)
[Prayers of special intention such as prayers for a holy day or the
Collect for the Order (see pp. 128-129) may be included.]

THE LORD'S PRAYER   *(See pp. 126-127)*

CONCLUDING COLLECT
   O most merciful Redeemer, friend and brother,
   may we know you more clearly,
   love you more dearly,
   and follow you more nearly,
   for your own sake. **Amen.**

Richard of Chichester, 13th c.

HYMN   87.87.87

Tune: PICARDY (*BOS* 25, *UMH* 626)
("Let all mortal flesh keep Silence")

Love will be our Lenten calling,
love to shake and shatter sin,
waking every closed, cold spirit,
stirring new life deep within,
'til the quickened heart remembers
what our Easter birth can mean.

Peace will be our Lenten living
as we turn for home again,
Longing for the words of pardon,
stripping off old grief and pain,
'til we stand, restored and joyful,
with the Church on Easter Day.

GOING FORTH

Blessings as we journey to
   the shadows and the cross and the grave
   and the fire and the book
   and the font and the table
   and the Life of all that lives.
May God bring us back to the place
that grace and penitence brought us
when we first believed.

DTB

The grace of the Lord Jesus Christ be with us.
   Let us bless the Lord. **Thanks be to God**.

evening prayer
for Lent

OPENING

ENTRANCE OF THE LIGHT

Jesus Christ, you are the light of the world,
the light no darkness can overcome.
Stay with us, for it is evening,
and the day is nearly over.
You said to our hearts: "Seek my face,"
and so it is your face we seek.

adapted from Psalm 27:8 *TIB*

HYMN OF LIGHT

(may be sung to psalm tone 1; for complete form see p. 130)
O gra-cious *Light,* *
pure brightness of our everlasting God in *heaven,*
O Je-sus *Christ,* * ho-ly and *blessed.*
Now as we come to the setting of the *sun,* *
and our eyes behold the ves-per *light,*
we sing your praises, O *God,* *
most holy and bless-ed *Trinity.*

Excerpted from "Phos hilaron," late 3rd/early 4th c.;
adapted by Timothy J. Crouch , O.S.L.
from the work of Charles Mortimer Guilbert

PRAYER OF AWARENESS AND ASSURANCE

(a recollection of Christ present in the moments of the day)
Great Spirit, you are always with us.
Therefore all that is now past,
we surrender to you with thanks;
all that is now present,
we receive from you with wonder;
all that is yet to be, we await from you with hope.
In all our days, you walk with us;
in all our hours, you dwell in us;
in all our years, you provide for us.
You are always with us, your baptized people,
through Lenten pilgrimage to Easter Joy. **Amen.**

Donald F. Chatfield, alt. Used with permission

Silence

May God who said, "Let light shine out of darkness,"
   shine in our hearts
to give us the light of the knowledge of the glory of God
   in the face of Jesus Christ.

Adapted from II Corinthians 4:6

We are a forgiven people! **Thanks be to God!**

PSALTER

PSALM

Out of the depths have I called to you;
   O God, <u>hear</u> my *voice,* *
the voice of my supplication,
   for there is for-<u>giveness</u> with *you.*

Adapted from Psalm 130:1-2, 4 OSH

(See pp. 100-107 or a psalm lectionary for additional psalter readings)

Glory to you, O Trinity, most <u>holy</u> and *blessed;* *
One God, now and for-<u>ever</u>. A-*men.***

SILENCE

WORD

[CANTICLE *(See p. 119)*]

SCRIPTURE

(see daily lectionary for additional appropriate readings, or)
We have been buried with Jesus through baptism,
and we joined with Jesus in death,
so that as Christ was raised from the dead
   by God's glory,
we too might live a new life.

Adapted from Romans 6:4 *TIB*

SILENCE

AN EXCERPT FROM THE CANTICLE OF MARY
(See p. 114 for complete form)
(may be chanted to psalm tone 2)

My soul proclaims your <u>great</u>-ness, *Lord;**
my spirit rejoices in <u>you</u>, my *Savior;*
You have mercy on <u>those</u> who *fear you**
in every <u>gen</u>-er-*ation.*
You have cast the mighty <u>from</u> their *thrones;**
you have lifted <u>up</u> the *lowly.*
You have filled the hungry <u>with</u> good *things;**
and the rich have been <u>sent a</u>-way *empty.*
You have come to the help of your <u>ser</u>-vant *Israel,**
for you have remembered your <u>promise</u> of *mercy*

TJC

[A READING FOR MEDITATION AND REFLECTION]

PRAYERS

Pray for the life of the church and the world and the concerns of the heart. (See p. 131.)
[Prayers of special intention such as prayers for a holy day or the Collect for the Order (see pp. 128-129) may be included.]

THE LORD'S PRAYER   *(See pp. 126-127)*
CONCLUDING COLLECT

Life of all that lives,
all the winter of our sins,
   long and dark, is flying;
all the summer of our frenzy,
   hot and bright, is passing:
and so, we give you laud and praise undying. **Amen.**
References to John of Damascus' hymn, "Come, ye faithful", DTB

HYMN   86.86 D CMD
Tune: KINGSFOLD (*BOS* 120, *UMH* 285)

On the dark road to Jerusalem,
Jesus, you set your face,
though knowing in your heart of hearts
could be your dying place.

36

You could not turn from cross's pain,
nor run from evil's power.
No other witness to God's reign,
but this courageous hour.

Our faith flows from your faithfulness,
our lives from your life-blood.
Against oppressive forces now
we walk the self-same road.
Your goodness is transforming strength,
your kin(g)dom earthly call.
We see beyond the terror tree,
life healing for us all.

Patricia J. Patterson, 2008. Used with permission.

GOING FORTH

The Lord Jesus be near us to defend us,
within us to refresh us, around us to preserve us,
before us to guide us, behind us to justify us,
and above us to bless us.

10th c. prayer adapted by TAR

The grace of the Lord Jesus Christ be with us.
Let us bless the Lord. **Thanks be to God**.

morning prayer
throughout the great fifty days
(easter through pentecost)

OPENING

CALL TO PRAISE AND PRAYER AND REMEMBRANCE OF BAPTISM

O God, open our lips,
> **and our mouths shall proclaim your praise.**

By Word and water God renews us this day
in the living fountain of God's grace
> **and raises us with Christ Jesus to live**
> **a new life in the Spirit.**

Remember your baptism and be thankful!
(water may be touched or poured)

AN EXCERPT FROM THE CANTICLE OF THE RESURRECTION

(Pascha nostrum; for the complete form, see p. 120)
(may be chanted to psalm tone 3)

Alleluia! Christ our Passover is sacri-<u>ficed</u> for *us;* *
therefore let us <u>keep</u> the *feast,*
not with the old leaven of <u>malice</u> and *evil,* *
but with the unleavened bread of sin-<u>cerity</u> and *truth.*
So consider yourselves <u>dead</u> to *sin* *
and alive to God in Jesus <u>Christ</u> our *Lord.*
For as in <u>Adam</u> all *die,* *
so also in Christ shall all be made alive. <u>Al</u>-le-*luia!*

I Corinthians 5:7-8 and Romans 6:9-11,
Text adapted from BCP, DTB, DWV

MORNING PRAYER

Hail, cross bearer and tomb breaker!
Hail, first born from the dead!
Hail, Spirit sender and life giver!
Hail, table host and joy of the world!
Our spirits awaken to your glory
and we rise up to meet you with our alleluias.
At the beginning of this new day,
set our hearts and minds to abide with you
until evening comes. **Amen.**

DTB

PSALTER

PSALM

Our God lives! Blessed <u>be</u> my *Rock!**
And let the God of my salvation <u>be</u> ex-*alted!*

Adapted from Psalm 18:46 TIB

(See pp. 90-98 or a psalm lectionary for additional psalter readings)

Glory to you, O Trinity, most <u>holy</u> and *blessed;**
One God, now and for-<u>ever</u>. A-*men*.

SILENCE

WORD

[CANTICLE *(See p. 121)*]

SCRIPTURE

(see daily lectionary for additional appropriate readings, or)
Christ is the beginning, the firstborn from the dead,
and so Christ is first in every way.
God wanted all things to be reconciled to God
    through Christ—
everything in heaven and everything on earth—
when Christ made peace by dying on the cross.

Selected from Colossians 1:18-20 TIB

Alleluia! Alleluia! Alleluia!

SILENCE

AN EXCERPT FROM THE CANTICLE OF ZECHARIAH
(See p. 112 for complete form)

(may be chanted to Psalm Tone 3)

We bless you, Adonai, <u>God</u> of *Israel,**
    for you come to visit us
    and ransom <u>us</u> from *bondage.*
You have brought forth a <u>strong</u> De-*liverer**
    in the house of <u>your</u> child, *David.*

Through your merciful compassions, <u>God</u> our *God,* *
the dawn from on <u>high</u> shall *visit us,*
to shine on those kept in dungeons
    and the <u>shadows</u> of *death**
and to guide our feet into the <u>paths</u> of *peace.*

TBE

[A READING FOR MEDITATION AND REFLECTION]

PRAYERS

Give thanks and pray for the coming day and the needs of the world.
    (See p. 131)
*[Prayers of special intention such as prayers for a holy day or the
Collect for the Order (see pp. 128-129) may be included.]*

THE LORD'S PRAYER   *(See pp. 126-127)*

CONCLUDING COLLECT
    Alleluia God, we rejoice in your dance from death
        which is the rhythm of our own resurrection.
    Thrill us with hope as we anticipate
        your promise of new life in the Spirit.
    Amen.

AMS

HYMN   76.76D
                        Tune: ST. KEVIN (*BOS* 122, *UMH* 315)
    Come, you faithful, raise the strain
    of triumphant gladness;
    God has brought forth Israel
    into joy from sadness;
    loosed from Pharaoh's bitter yoke
    Jacob's sons and daughters,
    led them with unmoistened foot
    through the Red Sea waters.

    "Alleluia!" now we cry
    to our King immortal.
    who, triumphant, burst the bars
    of the tomb's dark portal.

40

Come to glad Jerusalem,
who with true affection
welcomes in unwearied strains
Jesus' resurrection.

John of Damascus 8th c., trans. John Mason Neale, 1859 (alt.)

GOING FORTH

May the God of peace, who brought back from the dead
   our Lord Jesus, the great shepherd of the sheep,
by the blood of the eternal covenant,
make us complete in everything good
   so that we may do God's will,
   working among us that which is pleasing to God,
through Jesus Christ to whom be glory forever and
ever. **Amen**.

Hebrews 13:20-21 NRSV, alt.

The grace of the Lord Jesus Christ be with us.
Let us bless the Lord. **Thanks be to God**.
Alleluia!

41

evening prayer
throughout the great fifty days
(easter through pentecost)

OPENING

ENTRANCE OF THE LIGHT

> Jesus Christ, you are the light of the world,
> **the light no darkness can overcome.**
> Stay with us, for it is evening,
> **and the day is nearly over.**
> Holy Spirit, come and breathe within us,
> setting us on fire with your love. **Alleluia!**

HYMN OF LIGHT

> *(may be sung to psalm tone 1; for complete form see p. 130)*
> O gra-cious *Light,* *
> pure brightness of our everlasting God in *heaven,*
> O Je-sus *Christ,* * ho-ly and *blessed.*
> Now as we come to the setting of the *sun,* *
> and our eyes behold the ves-per *light,*
> we sing your praises, O *God,* *
> most holy and bless-ed *Trinity.*

> Excerpted from "Phos hilaron," late 3rd/early 4th c.;
> adapted by Timothy J. Crouch , O.S.L.
> from the work of Charles Mortimer Guilbert

PRAYER OF AWARENESS AND ASSURANCE

> *(a recollection of Christ present in the moments of the day)*
> Your light has filled our lives,
> but we hesitate to share it with others.
> **Lord, have mercy.**
> You have marked us as your own in baptism,
> but we have not lived as your faithful people.
> **Christ, have mercy.**
> You have called us to be a light to the nations,
> but we have hidden our light under a bushel.
> **Lord, have mercy.**

Transform us by the power of your Holy Spirit
so that we may live our baptism as your new creation,
forgiven and made whole by your matchless love.
Amen.

DWV

Silence

May God who said, "Let light shine out of darkness,"
    shine in our hearts
to give us the light of the knowledge of the glory of God
    in the face of Jesus Christ.

Adapted from II Corinthians 4:6

We are a forgiven people!
Thanks be to God! Alleluia!

PSALTER

PSALM

Alleluia! Praise ADO-<u>NAI</u>, my *soul!**
I will praise you all my life;
    I will sing praise to my God <u>while</u> I *live!*

Psalm 146:1-2 *TIB*

(See pp. 100-107 or a psalm lectionary for additional psalter readings)

Glory to you, O Trinity, most <u>holy</u> and *blessed;
One God, now and for-<u>ever</u>. A-*men*.

SILENCE

WORD

[CANTICLE *(See p. 122)*]

SCRIPTURE

(see daily lectionary for additional appropriate readings, or)
Jesus said:
If you love me and obey the command I give you,
I will ask the One who sent me
to give you another Paraclete, another Helper
to be with you always—the Spirit of truth.

John 14:15-17a *TIB*

Alleluia! Alleluia! Alleluia!

SILENCE

AN EXCERPT FROM THE CANTICLE OF MARY
(See p. 114 for complete form)
(may be chanted to psalm tone 2)
My soul proclaims your great-ness, *Lord;**
my spirit rejoices in you, my *Savior;*
You have mercy on those who *fear you**
in every gen-er-*ation.*
You have cast the mighty from their *thrones;**
you have lifted up the *lowly.*
You have filled the hungry with good *things;**
and the rich have been sent a-way *empty.*
You have come to the help of your ser-vant *Israel,**
for you have remembered your promise of *mercy.*

TJC

[A READING FOR MEDITATION AND REFLECTION]

PRAYERS

Pray for the life of the church and the world and the concerns of the heart. (See p. 131.)
[Prayers of special intention such as prayers for a holy day or the Collect for the Order (see pp. 128-129) may be included.]

THE LORD'S PRAYER   *(See pp. 126-127)*
CONCLUDING COLLECT
God of wind and word and fire,
send us the light of your Holy Spirit
that tongue and soul and mind and strength
may proclaim your praise.
Set our love aflame by the fire of your love,
and empower us with your presence
in the name of Christ. **Amen.**

Adapted from the Hymn for Terce
attributed to St. Ambrose (340-497)

HYMN   77.77
Tune: CANTERBURY (*BOS* 130, *UMH* 465)

Holy Spirit, Truth divine,
dawn upon this soul of mine;
Word of God and inward light,
wake my spirit, clear my sight.

Holy Spirit, Love divine,
glow within this heart of mine.
Be my Lord and I shall be
firmly bound, forever free.

Samuel Longfellow, 1864

GOING FORTH

The God of all grace, who has called us
    to eternal glory in Christ,
establish and strengthen us by the power
    of the Holy Spirit,
that we may live in grace and peace. **Amen.**

Adapted from I Peter 5:10, OSL

The grace of the Lord Jesus Christ be with us.
Let us bless the Lord.
Thanks be to God. Alleluia!

morning prayer
for ordinary time after pentecost

OPENING

CALL TO PRAISE AND PRAYER AND REMEMBRANCE OF BAPTISM

O God, open our lips,
and our mouths shall proclaim your praise.
By Word and water God renews us this day
in the living fountain of God's grace
**and raises us with Christ Jesus to live
a new life in the Spirit.**
Remember your baptism and be thankful!
(water may be touched or poured)

MORNING HYMN

88.88 LM
Tune: SPLENDOR PATERNAE (*BOS* 58)
or WAREHAM (*UMH* 679)

O splendor of God's glory bright,
eternal source of light from light,
O Light of light, light's living spring,
O Day, all days illumining.

To guide whate'er we seek to do,
with love all envy to subdue,
to make ill fortune turn to fair,
and give us grace our love to share.

Ambrose of Milan, 4th c.,
trans. Robert Bridges, 1899 alt.

MORNING PRAYER

Dawn from on high, your light illumines all our days.
Awaken us to your visitations throughout this day.
Be merciful in us for the sake of others.
Make us fearless when confronting injustice and need,
that we may give you glory in the power of the Spirit.
Amen.

DTB

PSALTER

PSALM

Turn your ear to me and <u>hear</u> my *prayer.* *
Show me your steadfast love and <u>your</u> great *strength.*
Guard me as the apple <u>of</u> your *eye;* *
hide me in the shadow <u>of</u> your *wings.*
When I look at justice, I <u>see</u> your *face,* *
when I awake I'm content just to <u>see</u> your *likeness.*

Selected from Psalm 17:6-8, 15 TIB

(See pp. 90-98 or a psalm lectionary for additional psalter readings)

Glory to you, O Trinity, most <u>holy</u> and *blessed;* *
One God, now and for-<u>ever</u>. A-*men*.

SILENCE

WORD

[CANTICLE *(See p. 123)*]

SCRIPTURE

(see daily lectionary for additional appropriate readings, or)
Do not be conformed to this world, but be transformed
by the renewing of your minds, so that you may discern
what is the will of God—what is good and acceptable
and perfect.

Romans 12:2 NRSV

SILENCE

AN EXCERPT FROM THE CANTICLE OF ZECHARIAH
(See p. 112 for complete form)
(may be chanted to Psalm Tone 3)
We bless you, Adonai, <u>God</u> of *Israel,* *
for you come to visit us
and ransom <u>us</u> from *bondage.*
You have brought forth a <u>strong</u> De-*liverer**
in the house of <u>your</u> child, *David.*
Through your merciful compassions, <u>God</u> our *God,* *

47

the dawn from on <u>high</u> shall *visit us,*
to shine on those kept in dungeons
   and the <u>shadows</u> of *death**
and to guide our feet into the <u>paths</u> of *peace.*

TBE

[A READING FOR MEDITATION AND REFLECTION]

PRAYERS

Give thanks and pray for the coming day and the needs of the world.
   (See pg. 131)
[Prayers of special intention such as prayers for a holy day or the
Collect for the Order (see pp. 128-129) may be included.]

THE LORD'S PRAYER   *(See pp. 126-127)*

Concluding Collect

Mighty and everlasting God,
who has safely brought us to the beginning of this day:
defend us with your mighty power,
and grant that this day we fall into no sin,
neither run into any kind of danger,
but that all our doings, ordered by your governance,
may be always pleasing in your sight,
through Jesus Christ our Lord. **Amen**.

BCP

HYMN   88.88 LM
Tune: TALLIS' CANON (*BOS* 61, *UMH* 682)

New every morning is the love
our wakening and uprising prove;
through sleep and darkness safely brought,
restored to life and power and thought.

The trivial round, the common task,
will furnish all we ought to ask,
if on our daily course our mind
be set to hallow all we find.

John Keble, 1822

48

GOING FORTH

Rejoice in the Lord always; again I say rejoice!
May the peace of God
   which passes all our understanding
guard our hearts and our minds in Christ Jesus.
Amen.

Adapted from Philippians 4:4-7 OSL

The grace of the Lord Jesus Christ be with us.
Let us bless the Lord. **Thanks be to God**.

evening prayer
for ordinary time after pentecost

OPENING

ENTRANCE OF THE LIGHT

>Jesus Christ, you are the light of the world,
>**the light no darkness can overcome.**
>Stay with us, for it is evening,
>**and the day is nearly over.**

HYMN OF LIGHT

>*(may be sung to psalm tone 1; for complete form see p. 130)*
>O gra-cious *Light,* *
>pure brightness of our everlasting God in *heaven,*
>O Je-sus *Christ,* * ho-ly and *blessed.*
>Now as we come to the setting of the *sun,* *
>and our eyes behold the ves-per *light,*
>we sing your praises, O *God,* *
>most holy and bless-ed *Trinity.*

Excerpted from "Phos hilaron," late 3rd/early 4th c.;
adapted by Timothy J. Crouch , O.S.L.
from the work of Charles Mortimer Guilbert

PRAYER OF AWARENESS AND ASSURANCE

>*(a recollection of Christ present in the moments of the day)*
>Merciful God:
>we have not loved you with our whole heart,
>nor our neighbors as ourselves.
>For the sake of Jesus Christ,
>forgive what we have been,
>accept us as we are,
>and guide what we shall be
>through Jesus Christ our Lord. **Amen**.

BCP 1979, alt

>*Silence*
>May God who said, "Let light shine out of darkness,"
>shine in our hearts to give us the light of the knowledge
>of the glory of God in the face of Jesus Christ.

Adapted from II Corinthians 4:6

>We are a forgiven people! **Thanks be to God!**

PSALTER

PSALM

You are my ever-burning lamp, A –DO-*NAI!**
My God, you <u>lighten</u> my *darkness!*
O God, your way is perfect;
    your promise, ADO-<u>NAI</u>, proves *true;**
you are a shield for all who take <u>refuge</u> in *you.*

Psalm 18:28,30 *TIB*

(See pp. 100-107 or a psalm lectionary for additional psalter readings)

Glory to you, O Trinity, most <u>holy</u> and *blessed;
One God, now and for-<u>ever</u>. A-*men*.**

SILENCE

WORD

[CANTICLE *(See p. 123)*]

SCRIPTURE
    (see daily lectionary for additional appropriate readings, or)
    The Lord says,
    "Come, everyone who is thirsty—here is water!
    Why spend money on what does not satisfy?
    Why spend your wages and still be hungry?
    Listen to me and do what I say,
        and you will enjoy the best food of all.

Isaiah 55:1a, 2 *TEV*

SILENCE

AN EXCERPT FROM THE CANTICLE OF MARY
    (See p. 114 for complete form)
                (may be chanted to psalm tone 2)
    My soul proclaims your <u>great</u>-ness, *Lord;**
    my spirit rejoices in <u>you</u>, my *Savior;*
    You have mercy on <u>those</u> who *fear you**
    in every <u>gen</u>-er-*ation.*

You have cast the mighty <u>from</u> their *thrones;* *
you have lifted <u>up</u> the *lowly.*
You have filled the hungry <u>with</u> good *things;* *
and the rich have been <u>sent a</u>-way *empty.*
You have come to the help of your <u>ser</u>-vant *Israel,* *
for you have remembered your <u>promise</u> of *mercy*

TJC

[A READING FOR MEDITATION AND REFLECTION]

PRAYERS

Pray for the life of the church and the world and the concerns of the heart. (See p. 131.)
[Prayers of special intention such as prayers for a holy day or the Collect for the Order (see pp. 128-129) may be included.]

THE LORD'S PRAYER   *(See pp. 126-127)*

CONCLUDING COLLECT

O God, the light of the minds who know you,
the life of the souls who love you,
and the strength of thoughts that seek you:
help us so to know you that we might truly love you,
and so to love you that we may truly serve you,
whose service is perfect freedom;
through Jesus Christ our Lord.
Amen.

Adapted from The Gelasian Sacramentary, 5th c.

HYMN   11.10 11.10
Tune: FINLANDIA, first two and last two lines (*UMH* 437)
or STRENGTH AND STAY *(BOS* 78)

O Strength and Stay upholding all creation,
who with us day and night ever abides;
yet day by day as light in due gradation
from hour to ho-ur changes, you still guide.

Grant to life's day a peaceful, faithful ending,
an eve untouched by shadows of decay,
the brightness of your grace at death be blending
with dawning glories of eternal day.

St. Ambrose, 340-97;
trans. John Ellerton, 1826-1893 and F. J. A. Hart, 1818-1892

GOING FORTH

Good Shepherd, bless your flock this night.
Give your peace, your help,
   your love to the sheep of your fold
that we may be united in peace and love
   as one body, one spirit,
in one hope of our calling
   through your boundless love. **Amen.**

Adapted from the Liturgy of Saint Mark, 4th c.

The grace of the Lord Jesus Christ be with us.
Let us bless the Lord. **Thanks be to God.**

morning prayer
for ordinary time before advent

OPENING

CALL TO PRAISE AND PRAYER AND REMEMBRANCE OF BAPTISM

O God, open our lips,
and our mouths shall proclaim your praise.
By Word and water God renews us this day
in the living fountain of God's grace
**and raises us with Christ Jesus to live
a new life in the Spirit.**
Remember your baptism and be thankful!
(water may be touched or poured)

MORNING HYMN

77.77.77
Tune: RATISBON
(*BOS* 57, *UMH* 173)

Christ, whose glory fills the skies,
Christ the true, the only light,
Son of Righteousness, arise,
triumph o'er the shades of night;
Dayspring from on high be near;
Daystar, in my heart appear.

Dark and cheerless is the morn
unaccompanied by thee;
joyless is the day's return,
till thy mercy's beams I see;
till they inward light impart,
cheer my eyes and warm my heart.

Charles Wesley, 1740

MORNING PRAYER

God, whose Word resounds in all the cosmos:
we rejoice to be and to believe.
Let your Word be in our hearts and in our actions.
Give yourself to others through us
and free us to embody your healing grace for all
creation. **Amen.**

DTB, alt.

PSALTER

Your love, ADONAI, reaches <u>to</u> the *heavens,* *
your faithfulness <u>to</u> the *skies.*
Whether human or animal, ADONAI,
   you keep us all <u>in</u> your *care.* *
How precious <u>is</u> your *love!*

Selected from Psalm 36:5-7 TIB

(See pp. 90-98 or a psalm lectionary for additional psalter readings)

Glory to you, O Trinity, most <u>holy</u> and *blessed;* *
One God, now and for-<u>ever</u>. A-*men*.

SILENCE

WORD

[CANTICLE *(See p. 124)*]

SCRIPTURE
(see daily lectionary for additional appropriate readings, or)
Christ is the image of the unseen God
   and the firstborn of all creation,
for in Christ were created all things in heaven
   and on earth:
everything visible and invisible,
Thrones, Dominations, Sovereignties, Powers --
all things were created through Christ and for Christ.
Before anything was created, Christ existed,
and all things hold together in Christ.

Colossians 1:15-17 TIB

SILENCE

AN EXCERPT FROM THE CANTICLE OF ZECHARIAH
(See p. 112 for complete form)
(may be chanted to Psalm Tone 3)
We bless you, Adonai, <u>God</u> of *Israel,* *
   for you come to visit us
   and ransom <u>us</u> from *bondage.*

55

You have brought forth a <u>strong</u> De-*liverer**
   in the house of <u>your</u> child, *David*.
Through your merciful compassions, <u>God</u> our *God,* *
the dawn from on <u>high</u> shall *visit us,*
to shine on those kept in dungeons
   and the <u>shadows</u> of *death**
and to guide our feet into the <u>paths</u> of *peace*.

TBE

[A READING FOR MEDITATION AND REFLECTION]

PRAYERS

Give thanks and pray for the coming day and the needs of the world.
   (See p. 131)
[Prayers of special intention such as prayers for a holy day or the
Collect for the Order (see pp. 128-129) may be included.]

THE LORD'S PRAYER   *(See pp. 126-127)*

CONCLUDING COLLECT
   God of wind, water, fire, and earth,
   you fill all creation with beauty
   and call us to share in your ministry of healing.
   May we cherish and use your gifts wisely,
   rejoicing that we are part of your creation.
   nurturing and sharing it
      as we serve you and one another
   in the name of Jesus Christ your Chosen One. **Amen.**

BCP, 1928; alt.

HYMN   87.87
Tune: HOLY MANNA (*UMH* 150)
or MUSICA MUNDANA (*BOS* 30)

   Planets humming as they wander,
   stars aflame with silent song.
   Galaxies are spinning endless
   melodies, afar but strong.
   God's creation tunes a timeless hymn
   as far as we can gaze.
   Heavenly bodies help us hear
   the universal song of praise.

Human voices praise our Maker,
part of the created choir:
rumbling tones of space below us,
neutron's descant ever higher.
Hymns arise from all around us,
thankful praise our whole life long,
to the One who made us, knows us,
Author of the endless song!

Heather Josselyn-Cranson, OSL, 2010

GOING FORTH

God be in my head, **and in my understanding.**
God be in my eyes, **and in my looking;**
God be in my mouth, **and in my speaking;**
God be in my heart, **and in my thinking;**
God be at my end, **and at my departing. Amen.**

A Sarum Primer, 1588 as used in
the early "Green Card Rite" of The Order of Saint Luke

The grace of the Lord Jesus Christ be with us.
Let us bless the Lord. **Thanks be to God.**

evening prayer
for ordinary time before advent

OPENING

ENTRANCE OF THE LIGHT

Jesus Christ, you are the light of the world,
the light no darkness can overcome.
Stay with us, for it is evening,
and the day is nearly over.

HYMN OF LIGHT

(may be sung to psalm tone 1; for complete form see p. 130)
O <u>gra</u>-cious *Light,* *
pure brightness of our everlasting <u>God</u> in *heaven,*
O <u>Je</u>-sus *Christ,* * ho-<u>ly</u> and *blessed.*
Now as we come to the setting <u>of</u> the *sun,* *
and our eyes behold the <u>ves</u>-per *light,*
we sing your <u>praises</u>, O *God,* *
most holy and <u>bless</u>-ed *Trinity.*

> Excerpted from "Phos hilaron," late 3rd/early 4th c.;
> adapted by Timothy J. Crouch , O.S.L.
> from the work of Charles Mortimer Guilbert

PRAYER OF AWARENESS AND ASSURANCE

(a recollection of Christ present in the moments of the day)
Maker of earth and sky:
put our hands and hearts
to what preserves the integrity, stability and beauty
of the fabric of creation.
In all ways that tend otherwise, thwart us
until we see ourselves one in the communion
of all things,
with Jesus Christ the Living Word,
through whom all things were made. **Amen**.

> DTB (Based on a text
> in Aldo Leopold's "The Land Ethic")

Silence

May God who said, "Let light shine out of darkness,"
   shine in our hearts
to give us the light of the knowledge of the glory of God
   in the face of Jesus Christ.

Adapted from II Corinthians 4:6

We are a forgiven people! **Thanks be to God!**

PSALTER

PSALM

ADONAI, what variety you <u>have</u> cre-*ated*, *
arranging every-<u>thing</u> so *wisely!*
The earth is filled with your <u>cre</u>- a -*tivity!**
May you find joy in <u>your</u> cre-*ation.*

Psalm 104:24, 31 TIB

*(See pp. 100-107 or a psalm lectionary for additional psalter
readings)*

Glory to you, O Trinity, most <u>holy</u> and *blessed;* *
One God, now and for-<u>ever</u>. A-*men*.

SILENCE

WORD

[CANTICLE *(See p. 124)*]

SCRIPTURE

(see daily lectionary for additional appropriate readings, or)
Through the Word all things came into being,
and apart from the Word
   nothing came into being that has come into being.
Of this, the Chosen One's fullness,
   we all have a share—gift on top of gift.

Adapted from John 1:3, 16 TIB

SILENCE

AN EXCERPT FROM THE CANTICLE OF MARY

(See p. 114 for complete form)

(may be chanted to psalm tone 2)

My soul proclaims your <u>great</u>-ness, *Lord;**
my spirit rejoices in <u>you</u>, my *Savior;*
You have mercy on <u>those</u> who *fear you**
in every <u>gen</u>-er-*ation.*
You have cast the mighty <u>from</u> their *thrones;**
you have lifted <u>up</u> the *lowly.*
You have filled the hungry <u>with</u> good *things;**
and the rich have been <u>sent</u> a-way *empty.*
You have come to the help of your <u>ser</u>-vant *Israel,**
for you have remembered your <u>promise</u> of *mercy*

TJC

[A READING FOR MEDITATION AND REFLECTION]

PRAYERS

Pray for the life of the church and the world and the concerns of the heart. (See p. 131.)
[Prayers of special intention such as prayers for a holy day or the Collect for the Order (see pp. 128-129) may be included.]

THE LORD'S PRAYER *(See pp. 126-127)*

CONCLUDING COLLECT

Great Spirit,
we thank you that all creation is connected
   in a web of grace.
Cause us to live in reverence that honors you
   and all you have created.
Blow through us even in the night hours,
   and prepare us to be channels of your healing love
      in all our choices and actions;
in the name of Christ the Healer we pray.
Amen.

DTB, DWV

HYMN   87.87.87
Tune: SICILIAN MARINERS (*BOS* 31, *UMH* 671)
("Lord, dismiss us with thy blessing")

Maker of the earth and ocean,
fill the world with harmonies.
God our dwelling in all ages,
giver of our families.
Draw us near you, lure us to you,
granting us a life that frees.

God our home and destination;
on the way we walk with thee,
giving visions, new creation,
sense of hope, community.
Draw us near you, lure us to you,
growing in a life that frees.

Patricia Patterson, 2007. Used with permission.

GOING FORTH

May the God of the cosmos quiet us,
the liberating freedom of the Word buoy us,
and the Holy Breath encompass and heal us
here and now and at every time and place. **Amen**.

DTB

The grace of the Lord Jesus Christ be with us.
Let us bless the Lord. **Thanks be to God**.

Diurnal (Daytime) Hours of Prayer

These brief offices punctuate the day with prayer. They are prayed in the setting in which we find ourselves, whether as an individual at work or re-creation, or as a community gathered for learning and fellowship or on retreat. While the traditional times for these offices are at the third, sixth, and ninth hours (that is, at 9:00 am, noon, and 3:00 pm), the exact time for each is variable according to the natural pattern of the context of the settings in which they are prayed. The time of silence at the beginning of each of these offices is an important part of the office itself.

mid-morning prayer
(Terce)

At the hour when the Holy Spirit came upon the Church at Pentecost we pray.

SILENCE
Be still, aware of God's presence within and around.

OPENING

O God, come to our assistance.
O Lord, hasten to help us.
Glory to the holy and blessed Trinity,
one God now and forever. Amen.

PRAYER

Holy Spirit,
come upon us this hour without delay;
pour out your graces on our souls.
Let tongue and soul and mind and strength
proclaim your praise.
Set our love aflame by the fire of your love,
and may its warmth enkindle love in our neighbors.
Empower us with your presence
in the name of Christ. **Amen.**

From the hymn for this hour
attributed to St. Ambrose, 340-397, alt.

PSALTER

(commonly sung to psalm tone 3 or said in unison)
Praise God, all you *nations,* *
laud the Most High, all you *peoples.*
(except during Lent:)
For God's loving-kindness toward us is *great,* *
and the faithfulness of God endures forever.
Al-le-*luia!*

(during Lent:)
For God's loving-kindness toward <u>us</u> is *great,* *
and the faithfulness of God en-<u>dures</u> for-*ever.*

Psalm 117, OSH

Glory to you, O Trinity, most <u>holy</u> and *blessed,* *
one God, now and for-<u>ever</u>. A-*men.*

THE LITTLE CHAPTER

God says to us:
I will draw you from far and near,
gather you from your exile
and bring you home.
I will wash you with fresh water,
and make you clean from all that defiles you.

I will give you a new heart,
and breathe a new spirit into you.
I will take away your heart of stone,
and give you a faithful spirit,
my own spirit to lead you
so that you may walk faithfully in my ways.
You will be my people
and I will be your God.

A canticle paraphrased from Ezekiel 36:24-28
OSL

SILENT OR SHARED PRAYER

THE LORD'S PRAYER

Our Father in heaven,
hallowed be your name,
your kingdom come,
your will be done, on earth as in heaven.
Give us today our daily bread.
Forgive us our sins
as we forgive those who sin against us.
Save us from the time of trial
and deliver us from evil.
For the kingdom, the power, and the glory are yours
now and forever. Amen.

ELLC

Concluding Prayer
> Living God,
> in whom we live and move and have our being,
> guide and govern us by your Holy Spirit,
> so that in all the cares and occupations of our life
> we may not forget you,
> but remember that we are ever walking in your sight;
> through Jesus Christ our Lord. **Amen.**

BCP, alt.

Let us bless the Lord!
Thanks be to God!

mid-day prayer

(Sext)

At the hour when Jesus was placed on the cross, we pray.

SILENCE
Be still, aware of God's presence within and around.

OPENING
O God, come to our assistance.
O Lord, hasten to help us.
Glory to the holy and blessed Trinity,
one God now and forever. Amen.

PRAYER
Risen Savior,
at this hour you hung upon the cross,
stretching out your loving arms.
Send your Holy Spirit into our hearts
to direct us in your way,
to comfort us in our afflictions,
and to lead us into all truth;
through Jesus Christ our Lord. **Amen.**

BCP, alt.

PSALTER
(commonly sung to psalm tone 4 or said in unison)
Give praise, you servants of *God.* *
Praise the name of the Most *High.*
Let God's name be *blessed**
from this time forth for ev-er-*more.*
From the rising of the sun to its go-ing *down,* *
let God's holy name be *praised!*

Psalm 113: 1-3 OSH

Glory to you, O Trinity, most holy and *blessed,* *
one God, now and for-ever. A-*men.*

67

THE LITTLE CHAPTER

Even the young may grow weak and fall exhausted,
but those who trust in God for help
  will find their strength renewed.
They will rise on wings like eagles.
They will run and not be weary;
when they walk, they will not grow weak.

A canticle paraphrased from Isaiah 40:30-31
OSL

SILENT OR SHARED PRAYER

THE LORD'S PRAYER

Our Father in heaven,
  hallowed be your name,
  your kingdom come,
  your will be done, on earth as in heaven.
Give us today our daily bread.
Forgive us our sins
  as we forgive those who sin against us.
Save us from the time of trial
  and deliver us from evil.
For the kingdom, the power, and the glory are yours
  now and forever. Amen.

ELLC

CONCLUDING PRAYER

Holy Wisdom, in your loving kindness you created us,
  restoring us when we were lost.
Inspire us with your truth,
  that we may love you with our whole minds
  and run to you with open hearts,
through Christ our Savior. **Amen.**

Alcuin of York, 8th c.

Send forth your Spirit, Lord.
  Renew the face of the earth.
Creator Spirit, come.
  Inflame our waiting hearts.

Lord, hear our prayer,
and let our cry come to You.
Let us bless the Lord!
Thanks be to God!

mid-afternoon prayer

(None)

At the hour when Jesus died on the cross, we pray.

SILENCE
Be still, aware of God's presence within and around.

OPENING

O God, come to our assistance.
O Lord, hasten to help us.
Glory to the holy and blessed Trinity,
one God, now and forever. Amen.

PRAYER

Living, loving God,
through your wisdom the hours of the day move on,
and there is yet much to do.
Keep us in your care and renew us with your strength,
so that we may not forget you
nor be unaware of your love towards those around us.
In the name of Christ
who lives and reigns with you and the Holy Spirit.
Amen

DWV

PSALTER

Happy are they who have not walked
in the <u>counsel</u> of the *wicked,* *
nor lingered in the way of sinners,
nor sat in the <u>seats</u> of the *scornful!*

Their delight is in the law of the <u>Ho</u>-ly *One,* *
and they meditate on God's law <u>day</u> and *night.*
They are like trees planted by streams of water,
bearing fruit in due season,
with leaves that <u>do</u> not *wither,* *
everything they <u>do</u> shall *prosper.*

It is not so <u>with</u> the *wicked;* *
they are like chaff which the wind <u>blows</u> a-*way.*

Therefore the wicked shall not stand upright
    when <u>judg</u>-ment *comes* *
nor the sinner in the council <u>of</u> the *righteous.*

For the Holy One knows the <u>way</u> of the *righteous,* *
but the way of the <u>wicked</u> is *doomed.*

Psalm 1 OSH, alt.

Glory to you, O Trinity, most <u>holy</u> and *blessed,*
one God, now and for-<u>ever</u>. A-*men.*

THE LITTLE CHAPTER

    Let each of us look out for the interests of one another,
        having the attitude that Christ Jesus had
    who, having the nature of God,
    did not seek to exploit equality with God,
        but emptied himself,
        taking the nature of a servant,
    becoming like us in human form,
    humbly walking the path of obedience
        all the way to death on the cross.

    Therefore, God lifted him high,
        giving him a name above all names,
    that at the name of Jesus
    our knees should bend and our tongues proclaim
    to the glory of God Most High:
    "Jesus Christ is Lord."

A canticle paraphrased from Philippians 2:6-11 OSL

SILENT PRAYER

THE LORD'S PRAYER

    Our Father in heaven,
        hallowed be your name,
        your kingdom come,
        your will be done, on earth as in heaven.
    Give us today our daily bread.

Forgive us our sins
    as we forgive those who sin against us.
Save us from the time of trial
    and deliver us from evil.
For the kingdom, the power, and the glory are yours
    now and forever. Amen.

ELLC

CONCLUDING PRAYER

Lord Jesus Christ, who came to set us free:
let the shadow of your cross fall upon us in this hour
that we may wonder at the gift of your redeeming love,
and be empowered by your Spirit
to take up our own cross daily and follow you. **Amen.**

DWV

Show us, O God, your mercy,
    and grant us your salvation.
Let us bless the Lord!
    Thanks be to God!

nocturnal

(night-time)

hours of prayer

compline

Compline is the office that "completes" the day. It has been called the "bedtime prayer of the Church." The mood of the entire office is one of peace and tranquility. Both speaking and singing are done quietly. The service begins and ends in silence.

SILENCE

Be still, aware of God's presence within and around.

CALL TO PRAYER

O God, come to our assistance.
O Lord, hasten to help us.
The Holy One grant us a restful night,
and peace at the last. **Amen.**

NIGHT HYMN

Advent, Christmas and Epiphany: 88.88 LM; CONDITOR ALME
(*BOS* 79, *UMH* 692)

Creator of the stars of night,
the people's everlasting light
O Christ, Redeemer of us all,
we pray you hear us when we call.

When this old world drew on toward night,
You came, but not in splendor bright,
not as a monarch, but the child
of Mary, blameless mother mild.

Latin, 9th c.

Lent and the Great Fifty Days: 6 6 11 D
DOWN AMPNEY (*BOS* 84, *UMH* 475)
Come down, O Love Divine, seek thou this soul of mine,
and visit it with thine own ardor glowing;
O Comforter, draw near, within my heart appear,
and kindle it, thy holy flame bestowing.

O let it freely burn, till earthly passions turn
to dust and ashes in its heat consuming;
let resurrection light shine in my darkest night,
and clothe me round, the while my path illuming.

Bianco of Siena, 1434,
trans. Richard F. Littledale, 1867, alt.

Ordinary Time   11 11 11.5
CHRISTE SANCTORUM (*UMH* 188, *BOS* 86)
("Christ is the World's Light")
Now, God be with us for the night is closing;
both light and darkness are of your disposing,
and 'neath your shadow, here to rest we yield us
for you will shield us.

O God, your name be praised, your kin-dom given.
Your will be done on earth as 'tis in heaven;
keep us in life, forgive our sins, deliver
now and forever.

Petrus Herbert, 1566, trans. Catherine Winkworth, 1863 alt.

CONFESSION AND ASSURANCE
O most Holy and Beloved,
our Companion, our Guide upon the way,
our bright evening star:
We repent the wrongs we have done.
We have wounded your love.
O God, heal us.
We stumble in the darkness.
Light of the world transfigure us.
We forget that we are your home.
Spirit of God, dwell in us.

Eternal Spirit, living God,
in whom we live and move and have our being,
all that we are, have been, and shall be
is known to you,
to the very secrets of our hearts
and all that rises to trouble us.

Living flame, burn into us,
cleansing wind, blow through us,
fountain of water, well up within us,
that we may love and praise
in deed and in truth.

Jim Cotter, *Prayer at Night*
Cairns Publications, 1991; used with permission

a time of silence-

We are a forgiven people! **Thanks be to God!**

PSALTER AND GLORIA
Our help is in the name of the Lord;
who made heaven and earth.

Psalm 139:1-11
(may be chanted to tone 2 or spoken softly and prayerfully)

O God, you have searched me <u>out</u> and *known me;**
you know my sitting down and my rising up;
you discern my thoughts <u>from</u> a-*far.*
You trace my journeys and my <u>rest</u>-ing *places,**
and are acquainted with <u>all</u> my *ways.*

Indeed, there is not a word <u>on</u> my *lips,**
But you, O God, know it <u>al</u>-to-*gether.*
You press upon me behind <u>and</u> be-*fore,**
and lay your <u>hand</u> u-*pon me.*

Such knowledge is too <u>wonderful</u> for *me;**
it is so high that I can-<u>not</u> at-*tain it.*
Where can I go then <u>from</u> your *Spirit,**
Where can I flee <u>from</u> your *presence?*

If I climb up to heaven, <u>you</u> are *there;**
if I make the grave my bed, you <u>are</u> there *also.*
If I take the wings of the morning
and dwell in the uttermost parts <u>of</u> the *sea,**
even there your hand will lead me,
and your right hand <u>hold</u> me *fast.*

(All)
If I say, "Surely the darkness will <u>co</u>-ver *me,* *
and the light around me <u>turn</u> to *night,"*
darkness is not dark to you;
  the night is as bright <u>as</u> the *day,* *
darkness and light to you are <u>both</u> a-*like*.

OSH Psalter

Glory to the holy and <u>bless</u>-ed *Trinity*,
one God, now and for-<u>ever</u>. A-*men*.

Silence

THE LITTLE CHAPTER

Advent/Christmas/Epiphany

The God who said: "Let light shine out of darkness" is the God who shines in our hearts with light, bringing us the radiance of the knowledge of the glory of God in the face of Jesus Christ. We have this treasure in common earthenware so that the incomparable power is clearly from God and not from us.

II Corinthians 4:6-7 OSL

Lent

Out of the rich treasures of divine glory, may God strengthen you inwardly with power through the Holy Spirit, and may Christ dwell in your hearts through faith, and as you are rooted and grounded in love, may you, with all the saints, be able to grasp and to know the breadth and length and height and depth of Christ's love that goes beyond all human understanding, so that you may be filled with all the fullness of God.

Ephesians 3:16-19 OSL

The Great Fifty Days

The God of peace, who brought back from the dead the great shepherd of the sheep in the blood of the eternal covenant, Jesus our Savior, furnish you with all that is good, so that you may do all that is pleasing to God. To Christ be glory forever! Amen.

Hebrews 13:20-21 *TIB*

Ordinary Time (the following or one of the above)

> Come to me, all who labor and carry heavy burdens and I will give you rest. Take my yoke upon you and learn from me, for I am gentle and humble in heart, and you will find rest for your souls, for my yoke is easy and my burden is light.

Matthew 11:28-30 OSL

Holy wisdom, holy word!
Thanks be to God!

Silence for Reflection

Prayers

The Kyrie

Lord, have mercy.	*or*	Kyrie, eleison.
Christ, have mercy.		**Christe, eleison,**
Lord, have mercy.		Kyrie, eleison.

Silent or Shared Prayers

Night Prayers

Day dies away,
yet your light shines on in the darkness.
As we pray at the ending of the day,
bring our work to a close,
and prepare us for rest and peace at the last. **Amen**.

DTB

Keep watch, dear Lord,
with those who work or watch or weep this night,
and give your angels charge over those who sleep.
Tend the sick, give rest to the weary, bless the dying,
soothe the suffering, comfort the afflicted,
  shield the joyous,
and all for your love's sake. **Amen.**

BCP

O Lord,
support us all the day long of this troublous life,
until the shadows lengthen and the evening comes,
and the busy world is hushed,
and the fever of life is over, and our work is done.
Then in your mercy grant us a safe lodging,
and a holy rest, and peace at the last. **Amen.**

John Henry Newman, 1801-1890

Concluding Prayer

As we remember the prayer Jesus taught us, we pray:
  Eternal Spirit,
  Life Giver, Pain Bearer, Love Maker,
  Source of all that is and that shall be,
  Father and Mother of us all,
  Loving God, in whom is heaven:
  The hallowing of your name
    echo through the universe!
  The way of your justice
    be followed by the peoples of the world!
  Your heavenly will be done by all created beings!
  Your commonwealth of peace and freedom
    sustain our hope and come on earth.

With the bread we need for today, feed us.
In the hurts we absorb from one another, forgive us.
In times of temptation and test, strengthen us.
From trials too great to endure, spare us.
From the grip of all that is evil, free us.

For you reign in the glory of the power that is love,
now and for ever. **Amen.**

Jim Cotter, *Prayer at Night*
Cairns Publications, 1991; used with permission

HYMN   84.84.888.4
                              Tune: *AR HYD Y NOS (BOS* 87, *UMH* 688)

God who made the earth and heaven,
darkness and light,
who the day for toil has given, for rest the night.
May thine angel guards defend us,
slumber sweet thy mercy send us,
holy dreams and hopes attend us
this live-long night.

When the constant sun returning unseals our eyes,
may we born anew like morning, to labor rise.
Gird us for the task that calls us,
let not ease and self enthrall us,
strong through thee whate'er befall us,
O God most wise!

Reginald Heber, 1783-1826

COMMENDATION

In peace we will lie down and sleep.
   In the Lord alone we safely rest.
Guide us waking, O Lord, and guard us sleeping,
   that awake we may watch with Christ,
   and asleep we may rest in peace.
May the divine help remain with us always.
   And with those who are absent from us.

- silence -

Into your hands, O Lord, I commend my spirit.
   For you have redeemed me, O Lord,
   O God of Truth.

Psalm 4:8 and 30:5
Adapted from *The Sarum Breviary*

CANTICLE OF SIMEON *(The Nunc Dimittis)*
(commonly sung in unison to psalm tone 1)
Lord, you have now set your <u>ser</u>vant *free**
to go in peace as <u>you</u> have *promised;*
for these eyes of mine have <u>seen</u> the *Savior,**
whom you have prepared for all the <u>world</u> to *see,*
a Light to en-<u>lighten</u> the *nations,**
and the glory of your <u>peo</u>-ple *Israel.*

Luke 2:29-32 ICET

Glory to you, O Trinity, most <u>holy</u> and *blessed,
one God, now and for-<u>ever</u>. A-*men.***

BLESSING
May the holy and blessed Trinity guard and bless us.
Let us bless the Lord. **Thanks be to God!**

81

Ʋigil

Vigils are times of watching and waiting, trusting the resurrection light that breaks forth within the mystery of darkness. These "wombs of silence" call our souls to be still and know God. We take time to sense the music of the spheres, the "song the morning stars began," and join with all creation, the heavenly host, and the Church through the ages in singing the praise of God.

On Saturday Evenings, a Resurrection Vigil supersedes Evening Prayer and Compline. The service may also be used in a midnight Vigil or as the basis of a Festive Evensong before a saint's day or a holy day. For the Great Vigils of Christmas, Epiphany, Easter and Pentecost, see other resources.

OPENING

ENTRANCE OF THE LIGHT
>Jesus Christ, you are the light of the world,
>>**the light no darkness can overcome.**
>In the depths of our darkness,
>>**you come to meet us,**
>>**surprising us with joy.**

CANTICLE
For a Saturday Evening Resurrection Vigil:
Canticle of the Resurrection *(Pascha nostrum)*
>*(commonly sung to psalm tone 3;*
>>*for complete form, see p. 120.*
>*in Lent: spoken, not sung, omitting the Alleluia.)*
>[Alleluia!] Christ our Passover is sacri-<u>ficed</u> for *us;* *
>therefore let us <u>keep</u> the *feast,*
>not with the old leaven of <u>malice</u> and *evil,* *
>but with the unleavened bread of sin-<u>cerity</u> and *truth.*
>So consider yourselves <u>dead</u> to *sin* *
>and alive to God in Jesus <u>Christ</u> our *Lord.*
>>>Adapted from I Corinthians 5:7-8 and Romans 6:9-11; BCP

For a Mid-Night Vigil:
>Psalm 95:1-7 *(Venite Exultemus)*, p. 94.

For Festive Evensong before a Saint's Day or Holy Day:
>Canticle of Creation *(Benedicite, omnia opera Domini)*, p. 124.

PRAYER

>Blessed are you, God of all times and places,
>continue to recreate and form us
>with the light of your love.
>Remembering Christ's incarnation, life, death and rising,
>we rejoice to have been born by water and the Spirit
>at the font, the womb of your Church.
>**All glory be to you**
>>**through Jesus Christ our risen Lord**
>
>**in the light of the life-giving love**
>**of the Holy Spirit**
>**now and unto ages of ages. Amen.**

OSL

PSALTER

PSALM

>Our God lives! Blessed <u>be</u> my Rock!
>And let the God of my sal<u>vation</u> be exalted!

Psalm 18:46 TIB

(See Psalm 27, p. 102 or a lectionary for additional psalter readings)

>**Glory to you, O Trinity, most holy and blessed;**
>**One God, now and forever. Amen.**

SILENCE

WORD

SCRIPTURE

>*(see daily lectionary for additional appropriate readings, or)*
>In baptism you were not only buried with Christ,
>>but also raised to life,

because you believed in the power of God
who raised Christ from the dead.

Colossians 2:12 TIB

Holy wisdom! Holy Word! **Thanks be to God!**

SILENCE

AN EXCERPT FROM THE CANTICLE OF THE HOLY TRINITY

(Te Deum Laudamus)

(See The Book of Offices and Services pg. 185 for complete form)

(may be sung to psalm tone 3)

You are God, we *praise you!**
You are the Lord, we ac-*claim you!*
You are the eternal God who has cre-*ated!**
All creation wor-ships *you!*

Throughout the world,
    your holy Church *ac-claims you:**
O God of majesty un-*bounded,*
Your Chosen One, worthy of all *worship,**
and the Holy Spirit, advocate and *guide.*

Christ, you overcame the sting of *death;**
You will come to be our *judge.*
Come help your people and bring us with your *saints**
to glory ev-er-*lasting.*

Selected from the Ambrosian Hymn, OSL

[A READING FOR MEDITATION AND REFLECTION]

PRAYERS

SILENT OR SHARED PRAYER
Pray for the life of the church and the world and the concerns of the heart. See p. 131.

The Spirit Prayer

As we remember the prayer Jesus taught us, we pray:
Eternal Spirit,
Life Giver, Pain Bearer, Love Maker,
Source of all that is and that shall be,
Father and Mother of us all,
Loving God, in whom is heaven:
The hallowing of your name
    echo through the universe!
The way of your justice
    be followed by the peoples of the world!
Your heavenly will be done by all created beings!
Your commonwealth of peace and freedom
    sustain our hope and come on earth.

With the bread we need for today, feed us.
In the hurts we absorb from one another, forgive us.
In times of temptation and test, strengthen us.
From trials too great to endure, spare us.
From the grip of all that is evil, free us.

For you reign in the glory of the power that is love,
now and for ever. Amen.

Jim Cotter, *Prayer at Night*
Cairns Publications, 1991; used with permission

Commendation *(when Compline is not prayed)*

In peace we will lie down and sleep.
In the Lord alone we safely rest.
Guide us waking, O Lord, and guard us sleeping,
that awake we may watch with Christ,
and asleep we may rest in peace.
May the divine help remain with us always.
And with those who are absent from us.
silence
Into your hands, O Lord, I commend my spirit.
For you have redeemed me,
O Lord, O God of truth.

Adapted from the Sarum Breviary; Psalm 4:8 and 30:5

CANTICLE OF THE REDEEMED *(p. 123)* or
CANTICLE OF SIMEON *(Nunc dimittis)*
(commonly spoken in unison or sung to psalm tone one)
Lord, you have now set your ser-vant free*
to go in peace as you have promised;
for these eyes of mine have seen the Savior*
whom you have prepared for all the world to see,
a Light to en-lighten the nations,*
and the glory of your peo-ple Israel.

GOING FORTH
O God, hear our prayer,
and let our cry come to you.
Listen to the prayers of your servants;
have mercy on us, Lord Jesus Christ.
Let us bless the Lord!
Thanks be to God!
May the souls of the faithful departed,
through the mercy of God, rest in peace.
Amen.

selections from

psalms

for
morning and evening
prayer

For psalm tone music, see p. 133.

For directions on chanting the psalm tones, see pp. 6-7.

Antiphons are said or sung in unison at the beginning and conclusion of the psalm.

Indented strophes may be said or sung by a second voice or group.

In the antiphons for the psalms, the text for the antiphon is printed in italics while the syllable(s) sung to the last note are not italicized: I will sing praises <u>to</u> your name.

selections from psalms

for

morning prayer

Psalm 46

Be still and know that I am God.*
I am your refuge and your strength.

1   God is our refuge and our *strength,**
who from of old has helped us in our dis-*tress.*

> 2   Therefore we fear *nothing–**
> even if the earth should open up in front of us
> and mountains plunge into the depths
> of the *sea,*
> 3   even if the earth's waters rage and *foam**
> and the mountains tumble with its *heaving.*

4   There is a river whose streams
gladden the city of *God,**
the holy dwelling of the Most *High.*
5   God is in its midst, it will nev-er *fall;**
God will help it at *daybreak.*

> 6   Though nations are in turmoil
> and em-pires *crumble,**
> God's voice resounds, and it melts the *earth.*
> 7   Mighty ADO-NAI is *with us–**
> our stronghold is the God of *Israel!*

8   Come, see what ADO-NAI has *done–**
God makes the earth *bounteous!*
9   God has put an end to war
from one end of the earth to the *other,**
breaking bows, splintering spears,
and setting chariots on *fire.*

10 Be still, and know that I am *God!**
 I will be exalted among the nations;
 I will be exalted up-on the *earth.*

11 Mighty ADO-NAI is *with us–**
 our stronghold is the God of *Israel!*

TIB

Psalm 63 (selected)

Tone 6 or 4

Because your love is better than life,
my lips will glory -fy you.*
In the morning I will sing glad songs of praise to you.
(BOS 62)

1 ADONAI, my God,
   you are the One I *seek.**
My soul thirsts for you,
   my body longs for *you*
in this dry and wear-y *land**
   where there is no *water.*

2 So I look to you in the sanctuary
   to see your power and *glory;**
3 because your love is better than life,
   my lips will glori-fy *you.*

4 And so I bless you while I *live;**
in your Name I lift up my *hands.*
5 [My soul will feast and be *filled,**
and I will sing and *praise you.]*

6 I remember you when I'm in *bed;**
   through sleepless nights I meditate on you
7 because you are my *help.*

In the shadow of your wings I sing for *joy.**
8 My soul clings to you;
   your mighty hand up-*holds me.*

TIB [alt.]

Psalm 91, 92 (selected)   Tone 5

It is good to proclaim your love in the morning!*
Your deeds fill me with joy!

91   (*BOS* 304)

1   You who dwell in the shelter of the Most High
         and pass the night in the <u>shadow</u> of Shad-*dai,* *
2   say: "ADONAI, my refuge and my mountain fortress,
         my God in <u>whom</u> I *trust!"*

   3   For ADONAI says: "I will rescue you
             <u>from</u> the *snare,* *
         and shield you from <u>poison</u>-ed *arrows.*
   4   I will cover you with my pinions;
             under my wings you <u>will</u> take *refuge;* *
         my faithful-<u>ness</u> will *shield you.*

14   Because you love me, I <u>will</u> de-*liver you;* *
     I will rescue you because you ac-<u>knowledge</u> my *Name.*
15   You will call upon me, and I will <u>an</u>-swer *you;* *
     I will be with you in trouble;
         I will deliver you and <u>hon</u>-or *you."*

92   (*Bonum est, BOS* 196)

   1   It is good to praise you, <u>A</u>-DO-*NAI,* *
         and celebrate your Name in <u>song</u>, Most *High*—
   2   to proclaim your love <u>in</u> the *morning* *
         and your fidelity through the watches <u>of</u> the *night.*

4   Your deeds, ADONAI, fill <u>me</u> with *joy;* *
     I shout in triumph over the work <u>of</u> your *hands.*

   5   How great are your works, <u>A</u>-DO-*NAI,* *
         How pro-<u>found</u> your *thoughts!*

                                                              TIB

Psalm 95 (selected)

Tone 3

(Venite exultemus, BOS 197)

You <u>are</u> our God,*
and we are the flock <u>under</u> your care.

1   Come, let us sing joyful-<u>ly</u> to *God!**
     Raise a shout to our rock, <u>our</u> de-*liverance!*
2   Let us come into God's presence <u>with</u> thanks-*giving,**
     and sing our <u>praises</u> with *joy.*

    3   For ADONAI is <u>a</u> great *God,**
       the great Ruler, a-<u>bove</u> all *gods.*
    4   O God, in your hands are the depths
        <u>of</u> the *earth,**
       and the mountain <u>peaks</u> are *yours.*

5   Yours is the sea, <u>for</u> you *made it,**
     the dry land as well, for <u>your</u> hands *formed it.*
6   Come, let us bow <u>down</u> in *worship;**
     let us kneel before ADO-<u>NAI</u>, our *Maker.*

    7   For you are our God,
       and we are the <u>people</u> you *shepherd,**
       the flock under your care—
        if only we would hear God's <u>voice</u> to-*day!*

TIB

Psalm 96

Proclaim God's salvation day af-ter day;*
declare God's glory to ev-ery people.

1 Sing to ADONAI a new song!
   Sing to ADONAI, all the *earth!**
2 Sing to ADONAI, bless God's *Name!*

   Proclaim God's salvation day af-ter *day;**
3 declare God's glory among the nations,
      God's marvels to ev-ery *people.*

4 ADONAI is great, most worthy of *praise,**
   ADONAI is to be revered a-bove all *gods.*
5 The gods of the nations are nothing,
      they don't ex-*ist—**
   but ADONAI cre-ated the *universe.*

   6 In God's presence are splendor and *majesty,**
      in God's sanctuary power and *beauty.*
   7 Pay tribute to ADONAI, you tribes
         of the *people;**
      pay tribute to the God of glory and *power.*

8 Pay tribute to the glorious Name of _A-DO-*NAI;**
   bring out the offering, and carry it in-to God's *courts.*
9 Worship ADONAI, ma-jestic in *holiness;**
   tremble in God's presence, all the *earth!*

   10 Say among the nations,
         "ADONAI reigns su-*preme!"**
      The world stands firm and unshakable:
         ADONAI will judge each nation
         with strict *justice.*

continued on pg. 96

11 Let the heavens be glad*;*
let the <u>earth</u> re-*joice;**
let the sea roar and all <u>that</u> it *holds!*

12 Let the fields exult and all <u>that</u> is *in them!**
Let all the trees of the forest sing for joy
13 at the presence of ADONAI, for <u>God</u> is *coming.*

(All)
God is coming to <u>rule</u> the *earth–**
to rule the world with justice
and its <u>peoples</u> with *truth!*

TIB

Psalm 100

Give thanks to God! Bless God's Name!*
We are God's people and the sheep of God's pasture.

1 Acclaim ADONAI with joy, all the *earth!**
2 Serve ADONAI with gladness!
   Enter into God's presence with a joy-ful *song!*

  3 Know that ADONAI is God!
     ADONAI made us, and we belong
     to the Cre-*ator;**
     we are God's people and the sheep
     of God's *pasture.*

4 Enter God's gates with thanksgiving
   and God's courts with *praise!**
Give thanks to God! Bless God's *Name!*

  5 For ADONAI is good;
     God's steadfast love en-dures for-*ever,**
     and God's faithfulness to all gen-er-*ations.*

TIB

Psalm 103 (selected)

Tone 5

Bless ADONAI, <u>all</u> cre-ation,*
bless ADO-<u>NAI</u>, my soul!

1   Bless ADONAI, my soul!
    All that is in me, bless God's <u>ho</u>-ly *Name!**
2   Bless ADONAI, my soul,
    and remember <u>all</u> God's *kindnesses!*

3   The One who forgives all your sins
        is the One who heals all <u>your</u> dis-*eases;**
4   the One who ransoms your life from the Pit
        is the One who crowns you
        with <u>love</u> and *tenderness.*

5   The One who fills your years <u>with</u> pros-*perity**
    also gives you an eagle's <u>youth</u>-ful *energy.*
6   How you love justice, <u>A</u>-DO-*NAI!**
    You are always on the side of <u>the</u> op-*pressed.*

7   You revealed your intentions to Moses,
        your <u>deeds</u> to *Israel.**
8   You are tender and compassionate, ADONAI–
        slow to anger, and <u>al</u>-ways *loving;*

9   your indignation doesn't en-<u>dure</u> for-*ever,**
    and your anger lasts only for <u>a</u> short *time.*
10 You never treat us as our <u>sins</u> de-*serve;**
    you don't repay us in kind for the in-<u>justices</u> we *do.*

11 For as high as heaven is a-<u>bove</u> the *earth,**
        so great is the love for those <u>who</u> re-*vere you.*
12 As far away as the east is <u>from</u> the *west,**
        that's how far you remove our <u>sins</u> from *us!*

13 As tenderly as parents <u>treat</u> their *children,**
    that's how tenderly you treat your worshipers,
    <u>A</u>-DO-*NAI!**

TIB

98

selections from psalms

for

evening prayer

Psalm 8

You have crowned us with <u>glory</u> and honor.*
You have made us responsible for the works
   <u>of</u> your hands,

1   ADONAI, our Sovereign,
       how majestic is your Name in <u>all</u> the *earth!**
   You have placed your glory a-<u>bove</u> the *heavens!*

   2   From the lips of infants and children
          you bring forth words of <u>power</u> and *praise,**
      to answer your adversaries
          and to silence the <u>hostile</u> and *vengeful.*

3   When I behold your heavens, the work <u>of</u> your *fingers,**
   the moon and the stars which you <u>set</u> in *place–*
4   what is humanity that you should be <u>mindful</u> of *us?**
   Who are we that you should <u>care</u> for *us?*
5   You have made us barely <u>less</u> than *God,**
   and crowned us with <u>glory</u> and *honor.**

   6   You have made us responsible
          for the works <u>of</u> your *hands,**
      putting all things <u>at</u> our *feet—*
   7   all sheep and oxen,
          yes, even the beasts <u>of</u> the *field,**
   8   the birds of the air, the fish of the sea
          and whatever swims the paths <u>of</u> the *seas.*

9   ADO-<u>NAI</u>, our *Sovereign,**
   how majestic is your Name in <u>all</u> the *earth!*

                                                              TIB

Psalm 23

ADONAI, you are my shepherd;*
you anoint my head with oil–
   my cup _o-ver--flows!*

1 ADONAI, you are my *shepherd–*
   I want no-thing *more.*
2 You let me lie down in green *meadows;*
   you lead me beside restful waters:
3   you re-fresh my *soul.*

      You guide me to lush *pastures*
      for the sake of your *Name.*
4   Even if I'm surrounded by shadows of Death,
         I fear no danger, for you are *with me.*
      Your rod and your staff–
         they give me *courage.*

5 You spread a table for me
      in the presence of my *enemies,*
   you anoint my head with oil–
      my cup _o-ver-*flows!*

6   Only goodness and love will follow me
         all the days of my *life,*
      and I will dwell in your house, ADONAI,
         for days with-out *end.*

TIB (alt.)

Psalm 27   (selected)   Tone 4

Teach me your way, O God of <u>my</u> sal -vation,*
and lead me on a straight path
   for you are my <u>on</u>-ly help.

1   ADONAI, you are my light, my salvation—
     whom <u>will</u> I *fear?**
You are the fortress of my life—
     of whom will I <u>be</u> a-*fraid?*

    2   When my enemies attack me,
       spreading vicious lies about me
       where-<u>ever</u> they *go,**
      they, my adversaries and foes,
       will <u>stumble</u> and *fall.*

3   Though an army mounts a siege against me,
     my heart <u>will</u> not *fear;**
though war break out against me,
     I will <u>still</u> be *confident.*

    4   One thing I ask of you, ADONAI,
       one <u>thing</u> I *seek:**
      that I may dwell in your house
       all the days <u>of</u> my *life,*
       to gaze <u>on</u> your *beauty**
      and to meditate <u>in</u> your *Temple.*

5   You will keep me safe in your shelter
     when <u>trouble</u> a-*rises,**
you will hide me under the cover <u>of</u> your *Tabernacle—*
you'll set me <u>on</u> a *rock,**
high and <u>out</u> of *reach.*

    6   Then I'll be able to hold <u>my</u> head *up,**
      even with my enemies sur-<u>round</u>-ing *me.*
      I will offer in your Tabernacle sacrifices
       <u>of</u> great *joy—**
      I'll sing and make music to you, <u>A</u>-DO-*NAI!*

7 Hear me when I call, <u>A</u>-DO-*NAI!**
Have mercy on me and <u>an</u>-swer *me!*
8 You say to my heart, "<u>Seek</u> my *face,*"*
and so it is your <u>face</u> I *seek!*

TIB

Psalm 51 (selected)

Tone 2

You want truth to live in my <u>inner</u>-most being.*
O God, have mercy on me; teach <u>me</u> your wisdom!

1   O God, have <u>mercy</u> on *me!**
Because of your love and your great compassion,
    wipe a-<u>way</u> my *faults;*
2   wash me clean <u>of</u> my *guilt;**
purify me <u>of</u> my *sin.*

    3   For I am aware <u>of</u> my *faults,**
      and have my sin constant-<u>ly</u> in *mind.*
    4   I sinned against <u>you</u> a-*lone,**
      and did what is evil <u>in</u> your *sight.*

8   Instill some joy and gladness <u>in</u>-to *me;**
let the bones you have crushed re-<u>joice</u> a-*gain.*
9   Turn your face <u>from</u> my *sins,**
and wipe out <u>all</u> my *guilt.*

    10   O God, create a clean <u>heart</u> in *me,**
      put into me a new and <u>stead</u>-fast *spirit;*
    11   do not banish me <u>from</u> your *presence,**
      do not deprive me of your <u>ho</u>-ly *Spirit!*

12   Be my savior again, re-<u>new</u> my *joy,**
keep my spirit <u>steady</u> and *willing;*

    13   I will teach trans-<u>gressors</u> your *ways,**
      and sinners will re-<u>turn</u> to *you.*

TIB

Psalm 85 (selected)   Tone 8 or 1

Love and faithful-ness have met;
justice and peace have em -braced.

7   Let us see your mercy, A-DO-*NAI,* *
and grant us your de-*liverance.*

    8   I will listen to what you have to say, ADONAI—
        a voice that speaks of *peace,* *
    peace for your people and your friends
        so long as they don't return to their *folly.*

9   Your salvation is near for those who re-*vere you**
and your glory will dwell in our *land.*
10   Love and faithfulness have *met;**
justice and peace have em-*braced.*

    11   Fidelity will sprout from the *earth**
    and justice will lean down from *heaven.*
    12   ADONAI will give us what is *good,* *
    and our land will yield its *harvest.*

13   Justice will march before you, A-DO-*NAI,* *
and peace will prepare the way for your *steps.*

TIB

105

My help comes from ADONAI,
  who made <u>heaven</u> and earth!*
The Guardian of Israel
  will never slumber, <u>nev</u>-er sleep!

1   I lift my eyes <u>to</u> the *mountains–**
from where will <u>my</u> help *come?*

2   My help comes from ADONAI,
  who made <u>heaven</u> and *earth!**

3   ADONAI won't let our footsteps slip:
  our Guardian <u>nev</u>-er *sleeps.*

4   The Guardian of Israel
  will never slumber, <u>nev</u>-er *sleep!**

5   ADONAI is our Guardian;
  ADONAI <u>is</u> our *shade:*
with God by our side,

6   the sun cannot overpower <u>us</u> by *day,**
nor the <u>moon</u> at *night.*

7   ADONAI guards us from harm,
  <u>guards</u> our *lives.**

8   ADONAI guards our leaving
  and our coming back,
  now <u>and</u> for-*ever.*

TIB

Psalm 142

I cry to you, ADONAI;
I have said, "You <u>are</u> my refuge,*
when my spirit faints within me,
it is you who <u>knows</u> my way.

1   With all my voice, I cry to you, A-DO-*NAI!**
    With all my voice I <u>cry</u> for *mercy!*
2   I pour out my di-<u>stress</u> be-*fore you,**
    I tell you <u>all</u> my *troubles.*

3   When my spirit faints within me,
    it is you who <u>knows</u> my *way.**
    On the path I walk
    they have hidden a snare <u>to</u> en-*trap me.*

4   Look—there is no one beside me now,
    no one who <u>stands</u> with *me.**
    I have no place of refuge,
    no one to care a-<u>bout</u> my *life.*

5   I cry to you, ADONAI;
    I have said, "You <u>are</u> my *refuge,**
    all I have in the land <u>of</u> the *living."*

6   Listen, then, to my cry,
    for I am in the depths <u>of</u> des-*pair.**
    Rescue me from those who pursue me,
    for they are <u>stronger</u> than *I.*

7   Set me free from this prison
    so that your Name <u>may</u> be *praised.**
    The just will assemble around me
    because of your <u>goodness</u> to *me.*

TIB

canticles

As we pray the hours, canticles are at the heart of the Church's song. Whether said or sung, they are soul music for our communal prayer. Canticles speak both to us and for us through corporate acts of prayer or affirmation. Although they have neither rhyme nor meter, they are the earliest and most lasting hymns of the Church. We have included the Latin by which they are known as a reminder that when we use them, we join the Church through the ages and around the world.

Evangelical Canticles are those that come from the gospel of Luke the evangelist and have historic ties with specific hours in the Western Church: Benedictus at Morning Prayer, Magnificat at Evening Prayer, and Nunc dimittis at Compline. While appearing earlier as excerpts, we provide them here in their complete form and commend their use.

We have also selected **Seasonal Canticles** to form and express our spirituality as we pray through the seasons in the church year.

- A canticle may be a hinge between the psalter and the scripture lection in Morning and/or Evening Prayer, paralleling the way in which the evangelical canticles respond to scripture readings. This use is indicated in the text by brackets, indicating its optional use, i.e. [Canticle].
- If two scripture lections are read, the seasonal canticle may act as a response to the first and the evangelical canticle as a response to the second.
- A canticle may be understood as a proclamation of scripture, providing an additional or alternative reading for the hour.
- A canticle may serve as a response to the Little Chapter in one of the diurnal hours or at Compline.

They are pointed so they may be chanted to a psalm tone. Alternate strophes are indented so they may be said or sung antiphonally. Some may choose to chant the psalm and speak the canticle, others to speak the psalm and chant the canticle, and still others, to chant both. Those for whom chanting is difficult, especially when prayed alone, may open their souls to do the singing, even as their lips do the speaking.

May the Holy Spirit enable these canticles to seep into the marrow of our souls, forming us more completely in a Lukan spirituality. In time may we realize that we do not so much sing the canticles as find that the canticles sing us!

canticle of zechariah

(Benedictus)   *(Morning Prayer)*
                                             Tone 3

We bless you, Adonai, <u>God</u> of *Israel,* *
for you come to visit us and ransom <u>us</u> from *bondage.*
You have brought forth a <u>strong</u> De-*liverer* *
in the house of <u>your</u> child, *David.*

This is what your holy <u>prophets</u> an-*nounced:* *
deliverance from enemies
     and from the hand of <u>all</u> who *hate us;*
mercy a-<u>mong</u> our *ancestors,* *
and remembrance of your <u>ho</u>-ly *covenant.*

This is the solemn oath you swore to our <u>an</u>-cestor *Abraham,* *
to make us <u>un</u>-a-*fraid,*
to rescue us <u>from</u> our *enemies,* *
to serve before you, holy and just,
  all the days <u>of</u> our *lives.*

And this my little child, shall be called prophet
     of <u>the</u> Most *High,* *
going before you, Adonai, to pre-<u>pare</u> your *paths.*
He will make your people <u>know</u> de-*liverance* *
by the forgiveness <u>of</u> their *sins.*

Through your merciful compassions, <u>God</u> our *God,* *
the dawn from on <u>high</u> shall *visit us,*
to shine on those kept in dungeons
     and the <u>shadows</u> of *death* *
and to guide our feet into the <u>paths</u> of *peace.*

Luke 1:67-79 TBE

[All:]
Glory be to you,
  O Trinity most <u>holy</u> and *blessed,* *
who is now, ever was and ever shall be
     unto endless <u>ages</u>. A-*men.*

(On holy days:)
Glory to God: Source of all, Eternal Word and <u>Ho</u>-ly *Spirit,* *
one God, holy and <u>bless</u>-ed *Trinity,*
who is now, ever was and <u>ever</u> shall *be**
unto endless <u>ages</u>. A-*men.*

canticle of mary

(Magnificat)   *(Evening Prayer)*
                                                          Tone 2

My soul proclaims your <u>great</u>-ness, *Lord;* *
my spirit rejoices in <u>you</u>, my *Savior;*
For you have looked with favor on your <u>low</u>-ly *servant,* *
from this day all generations will <u>call</u> me *blessed.*

      You the Almighty have done great <u>things</u> for *me,* *
        and Holy <u>is</u> your *Name.*
      Your have mercy on <u>those</u> who *fear you* *
      in every <u>gen</u>-er-*ation.*

You have shown the strength <u>of</u> your *arm;* *
you have scattered the proud in <u>their</u> con-*ceit.*
You have cast the mighty <u>from</u> their *thrones;* *
you have lifted <u>up</u> the *lowly.*

      You have filled the hungry <u>with</u> good *things;* *
      and the rich have been <u>sent a</u>-way *empty.*
      You have come to the help of your <u>ser</u>-vant *Israel,* *
      for you have remembered your <u>promise</u> of *mercy,*
      the promise you made <u>to</u> our *forebears,* *
      to Abraham and his <u>children</u> for *ever.*

Luke 1:46-55 TJC, OSL

[All:]
Glory be to you,
  O Trinity most <u>holy</u> and *blessed,* *
who is now, ever was and ever shall be
  unto endless <u>ages</u>. A-*men.*

(On holy days:)
Glory to God: Source of all, Eternal Word and <u>Ho</u>-ly *Spirit,* *
one God, holy and <u>bless</u>-ed *Trinity,*
who is now, ever was and <u>ever</u> shall *be* *
unto endless <u>ages</u>. A-*men.*

114

canticle of simeon

(Nunc dimittis)

(Compline)
Tone 1

Now, Lord, you let your servant <u>go</u> in *peace:* *
your word has <u>been</u> ful-*filled.*
My own eyes have seen <u>the</u> sal-*vation* *
which you have prepared in the sight of <u>ev</u>-ery *people:*
a light to reveal you <u>to</u> the *nations* *
and the glory of your <u>peo</u>-ple *Israel.*

Luke 2:29-32 ELLC

Glory be to you,
   O Trinity most <u>holy</u> and *blessed,* *
who is now, ever was and ever shall be
   unto endless <u>ages</u>. A-*men.*

(On holy days:)
Glory to God: Source of all, Eternal Word and <u>Ho</u>-ly *Spirit,* *
   one God, holy and <u>bless</u>-ed *Trinity,*
who is now, ever was and <u>ever</u> shall *be* *
   unto endless <u>ages</u>. A-*men.*

.

second canticle of isaiah

(Quaerite Dominum)   *(Advent)*
                                                           Tone 5

"Seek me while I <u>may</u> be *found;**
call upon me while <u>I</u> am *near.*
Let wicked ones forsake their <u>way</u> of *life**
and sinners their <u>ways</u> of *thinking.*

    Let them return to me so I may have <u>mercy</u> on *them,**
    to your God because I a-<u>bundant</u>-ly *pardon.*
    My thoughts are <u>not</u> your *thoughts,**
    neither are your <u>ways</u> my *ways.*

As heaven is <u>higher</u> than *earth,**
my ways are higher <u>than</u> your *ways;*
so also <u>are</u> my *thoughts**
higher <u>than</u> your *thoughts.*

    As rain and snow fall from heaven
       and do not <u>re</u>-turn *there,**
    but water the earth, causing it <u>to</u> be *fruitful*—
    producing seed <u>for</u> the *sower**
    and food <u>for</u> the *eater*—

so my word, which goes forth <u>from</u> my *mouth,**
does not return <u>to</u> me *empty,*
but accomplishes <u>what</u> I *will**
and succeeds in what I send <u>it</u> to *do.*

    With joy you <u>will</u> go *out,**
    and in peace you will <u>be</u> led *forth.*
    Before you, the mountains and the hills will break out
       in <u>joy</u>-ous *praise;**
    And all the trees of the field will <u>clap</u> their *hands.*

Paraphrased from the Hebrew, Isaiah 55:6-12 CAB OSL

third canticle of isaiah

(Surge, illuminare)　　　　　　　　*(Twelve Days of Christmas*
and Feast of the Epiphany)
Tone 7 or 5

Arise, shine, for your <u>light</u> has *come!**
The glory of ADONAI is <u>rising</u> u-*pon you!*

　　　Though darkness still <u>covers</u> the *earth**
　　　and dense clouds en-<u>shroud</u> the *peoples,*
　　　upon you ADO-<u>NAI</u> now *dawns,**
　　　and God's glory will be <u>seen</u> a-*mong you!*

The nations will come <u>to</u> your *light**
and the leaders to <u>your</u> bright *dawn!*
Your gates will be open <u>night</u> and *day*—*
they will <u>never</u> be *shut.*

　　　They will call you City of <u>A</u>-DO-*NAI,**
　　　Zion of the Holy <u>One</u> of *Israel.*
　　　Never again will the sounds of violence
　　　　　be heard <u>in</u> your *land;**
　　　never again will there be devastation
　　　　　and destruction within <u>your</u> fron-*tiers.*

You will name your walls Liberation
　　and <u>your</u> gates *Praise.**
Never again will the sun <u>light</u> your *day;*
never again will the brightness of the moon
　　<u>light</u> your *night.**
For ADONAI will be your everlasting light;
　　your God will <u>be</u> your *glory.*

Traditional selections from Isaiah 60:1-22 *TIB*

canticle of wisdom

(Sapientia aedificavit sibi domum)

*(Ordinary Time
after Epiphany)
Tone 2 or 7*

Wisdom has built her house, setting up <u>sev</u>-en *pillars.* *
She has prepared the food and wine and <u>set</u> her *table.*
She has sent <u>out</u> her *servants* *
to call out from the heights a-<u>bove</u> the *city:*

    "Let those who want en-<u>lighten</u>-ment *come.* "*
    Come, taste my bread
      and drink the wine I have pre-<u>pared</u> for *you.*
    Give up your foolish-<u>ness</u> and *live,* *
    and walk the path of <u>un</u>-der-*standing.* "

If you are wise, your re-<u>ward</u> is *wisdom;* *
if you teach the just, they grow in <u>un</u>-der-*standing.*

    Wisdom begins with <u>reverence</u> for *God,* *
    and knowledge of the Holy <u>One</u> is *insight.*

A paraphrase adapted from Proverbs 9:1-6, 9-10 OSL

canticle of Redemption

(De profundis)

(Lent)
Tone 4

Out of the depths I cry to you, _A-DO-*NAI!**
God, hear my *voice!*
Let your ears be at-*tentive**
to my voice, my cries for *mercy!*

    If you kept track of our sins, _A-DO-*NAI,**
    who could stand be-*fore you?*
    But with you is for-*giveness,*
    and for this we re-*vere you.*

So I wait for you, ADONAI, my soul *waits,**
and in your word I place my *trust.*
My soul longs for you, ADONAI,
  more than sentinels long for the *dawn,**
more than sentinels long for the *dawn.*

    Israel, put your hope in _A-DO-*NAI,**
    for with ADONAI is a-bun-dant *love,*
    With ADONAI is the fullness of de-*liverance.**
    God will deliver Israel from all its *failings.*

Psalm 130 *TIB, alt.*

cαnticle of the Resurrection

(Pascha nostrum)

Tone 3

(spoken in Lent, omitting the Alleluia's)

[Alleluia!] Christ our Passover is sacri-<u>ficed</u> for *us;**
therefore let us <u>keep</u> the *feast,*
not with the old leaven of <u>malice</u> and *evil,**
but with the unleavened bread of sin-<u>cerity</u> and *truth*.

Christ being raised from the dead
   will never <u>die</u> a-*gain;**
death no longer has dominion <u>_o</u>-ver *him*.
The death he died, he died to sin, <u>once</u> for *all,**
but the life he lives, he <u>lives</u> to *God*.

So consider yourselves <u>dead</u> to *sin**
and alive to God in Jesus <u>Christ</u> our *Lord*.
For as in <u>Adam</u> all *die,**
so also in Christ shall all be <u>made</u> a-*live.**

I Corinthians 5:7-8 and Romans 6:9-11
Text adapted from BCP: DWV, DTB

120

canticle of acclamation

(Tu Christe Rex Gloriae)

You, Christ, <u>reign</u> in *glory,* *
the eternal Chosen <u>One</u> of *God.*
When you came in the flesh to <u>set</u> us *free,* *
you took our nature on you,
   human child of <u>hu</u>-man *mother.*

     To give us life, you died and
       <u>broke</u> death's *power,* *
     making us worthy by your <u>bound</u>-less *goodness.*
     You broke the chains that <u>held</u> us *captive**
     and opened wide the gates
       of eternal <u>life</u> with *you.*

O creator God, of majes-<u>ty</u> un-*bounded,* *
your Chosen One, worthy <u>of</u> all *worship:*
and the Holy Spirit, <u>advocate</u> and *guide,* *
save your people, and bless <u>your</u> in-*heritance.*

     Complete the work of <u>our</u> sal-*vation;* *
     with grace and judgment,
       come and <u>save</u> your *people.*
     And bring us <u>with</u> your *saints**
     to live with you in God's e-<u>ter</u>-nal *presence.*

Adapted from the closing strophes of the "Ambrosian hymn"
Attr. to Bishop Nicetus of Remesiana, c. 335-414,
Third strophe, *ELLC,* alt.

first canticle of isaiah

(Ecce Deus salvator)

(Evening Prayer during
The Great Fifty Days)
Tone 7 or 4

You, O God, are <u>my</u> sal-*vation!**
I am not afraid for I <u>trust</u> in *you!*
Indeed, you are my strength and my <u>song</u>, O *God!**
You have become <u>my</u> sal-*vation!*

    With joy you will draw water
      from the wells <u>of</u> sal-*vation.**
    On that day you will say,
      "Give thanks and call u-<u>pon</u> GOD's *name!*
    Make GOD's deeds known a-<u>mong</u> the *nations!**
    Declare that GOD's name <u>is</u> ex-*alted!"*

(All)
Sing to God, who has ac-<u>complished</u> great *things!**
May this be made known throughout <u>the</u> whole *earth!*
Cry aloud and sing for joy, O <u>Zi</u>-on-*dweller;**
for the Holy One of Israel is great <u>in</u> your *midst!*

Translated from the Hebrew: Isaiah 12:2-6 CAB OSL

122

canticle of the redeemed

(Magna et mirabilia) *(Ordinary Time after Pentecost)*
Tone 6 or 3

Great and marvelous <u>are</u> your *works,* *
mighty God <u>of</u> the *ages.*
Just and true <u>are</u> your *ways**
among <u>all</u> the *nations.*

> Who can fail to revere and glorify your name,
> <u>A</u>-do-*nai,* *
> for you a-<u>lone</u> are *holy?*
> From nations throughout the world
> we draw near and <u>wor</u>-ship *you,* *
> for your just and holy ways
> have <u>been</u> re-*vealed.*

(All)
To you, O God, u-<u>pon</u> the *throne,* *
to Christ the Lamb, and to the <u>Ho</u>-ly *Spirit*
be worship and praise, <u>power</u> and *glory,* *
now and unto ages of <u>ages.</u> A-*men.*

Adapted from Revelation 15:2-3 and 5:13 OSL
(Excerpt from The Canticle to the Lamb)

cɑɒticle of cɾeɑtioɒ

(Benedicite, omnia opera Domini)   *(Ordinary Time*
                                                              before Advent)
                                                              Tone 7 or 4

All you works of the Most *High,**
praise and exalt God above all for-*ever!*
        Sun and moon, stars in the *sky,**
        praise and exalt God above all for-*ever!*

Fire and heat, cold and *chill,**
praise and exalt God above all for-*ever!*
        Dew and rain, frost and *cold,**
        praise and exalt God above all for-*ever!*

Night and day, light and *darkness,**
praise and exalt God above all for-*ever!*
        Mountains and hills, seas and *rivers,**
        praise and exalt God above all for-*ever!*

Animals, wild and tame,
    dolphins and everything that lives in the *water,**
praise and exalt God above all for-*ever!*
        Servants of God, faithful men and women
            ever-y-*where,**
        praise and exalt God above all for-*ever!*

Souls of the faith-ful de-*parted,**
praise and exalt God above all for-*ever!*
        Saints and holy people of hum-ble *heart,**
        praise and exalt God above all for-*ever!*

(All)
People of God, give thanks
    for God's ever-last-ing *love;**
praise and exalt God above all for-*ever!*

Adapted from Daniel 3:57-87 *TIB*
(Song of the Three Young Men)

prayers

THE LORD'S PRAYER

Our Father in heaven,
   hallowed be your name,
   your kingdom come,
   your will be done, on earth as in heaven.
Give us today our daily bread.
Forgive us our sins
   as we forgive those who sin against us.
Save us from the time of trial
   and deliver us from evil.
For the kingdom, the power, and the glory are yours
   now and forever. Amen.

ELLC

THE SPIRIT PRAYER

As we remember the prayer Jesus taught us, we pray:

Eternal Spirit,
Life Giver, Pain Bearer, Love Maker,
Source of all that is and that shall be,
Father and Mother of us all,
Loving God, in whom is heaven:

The hallowing of your name
  echo through the universe!
The way of your justice
  be followed by the peoples of the world!
Your heavenly will be done by all created beings!
Your commonwealth of peace and freedom
  sustain our hope and come on earth.

With the bread we need for today, feed us.
In the hurts we absorb from one another, forgive us.
In times of temptation and test, strengthen us.
From trials too great to endure, spare us.
From the grip of all that is evil, free us.

For you reign in the glory of the power that is love,
now and for ever. Amen.

Jim Cotter, *Prayer at Night*
Cairns Publications, 1991; used with permission

COLLECT FOR THE ORDER OF SAINT LUKE

O Shepherd of us all,
    who inspired your servant Saint Luke the Physician
    to set forth in the gospel
    the love and healing power of Jesus:
Grant, we ask you, your Spirit to the Order of Saint Luke,
    that we may proclaim the Apostolic hope,
    magnify the Sacraments,
    and embody Christ's healing grace for all creation;
    through Jesus Christ our Lord. Amen.

OSL

INTERCESSIONS FOR THE ORDER OF SAINT LUKE *(for optional use following the collect for the Order)*

Hear our prayer and let our cry come to you
for *Brother/Sister (first name)* our abbot,
for the officers of the General Chapter,
for our priors,
   [or for *Brother/Sister (first name)* our prior]
for our brothers and sisters in the Order
   (especially . . .),
for a sense of community with others in the Order,
for grace to live for you and with each other
as we live our Rule of Life and Service.
Merciful God,
   hear our prayer.

OSL

ON A SAINT'S DAY

Praise to you, O God, for the memory of
  (name of saint),
and for saints who are with us today.
Witnesses in faith, in prayer, and in deed,
holy in life, perfected in love,
with us on earth, around us in heaven,
your faithful saints point the Way
from generation to generation. **Amen.**

OSL

ON MARIAN FEASTS

Blessed are you, God of all grace,
for in Jesus Christ you are our light and our life;
to you be glory and praise forever.
You gave your living Word to Mary, Birth Giver,
that through the Holy Spirit
she might bear the Word made flesh,
who brings light out of darkness,
and with your Spirit renews the face of the earth.
All praise and thanks to you,
most holy and blessed Trinity,
one God, now and for ages of ages. **Amen.**

DWV, OSL

HYMN OF LIGHT *(The "Phos hilaron")*
(commonly sung in unison to psalm tone 1)

O gra-cious *Light,* *
pure brightness of our everlasting God in *heaven.*
O Je-sus *Christ,* *
ho-ly and *blessed.*

Now as we come to the setting of the *sun,* *
and our eyes behold the ves-per *light,*
we sing your praises, O *God,**
most holy and bless-ed *Trinity.*

You are worthy at all *times,* *
to be praised by hap-py *voices,*
O Son of God, O Giver of *Life,* *
and to be glorified through all the *worlds.*

Phos hilaron, late 3rd/early 4th c.;
adapted by Timothy J. Crouch, OSL
from the work of Charles Mortimer Gulbert

PRAYERS OF SUPPLICATION AND INTERCESSION

Let us pray for
  those who suffer or are in trouble . . .
  the concerns of this local community . . .
  the world, its peoples and leaders . . .
  the life and mission of the Church . . .
  the earth and all its creatures . . .
  the concerns of our hearts . . .
  and the communion of the saints . . .

OSL

Show us your mercy, O Lord;
  and grant us your salvation.
Clothe your ministers with righteousness;
  let your people sing with joy.
Give peace, O Lord, in all the world;
  for only in you can we live in safety.
Lord, keep this nation under your care;
  and guide us in the way of justice and truth.
Let your way be known upon earth;
  your saving health among all nations.
Let not the needy, O Lord, be forgotten;
  nor the hope of the poor be taken away.
Create in us clean hearts, O God;
  and sustain us with your Holy Spirit.

BCP

COMMENDATION

"Life is short and we have never too much time for gladdening the hearts of those who are traveling the journey with us. Oh, be swift to love, make haste to be kind!"* For the joyous light of our Lord Jesus Christ and the love of God and the sustaining community of the Holy Spirit is with us, now and unto ages of ages. **Amen**.

*These words of Henri-Frederic Amiel (1821-1881) were used by Chaplain General Timothy J. Crouch, OSL, in his valedictory benediction to the Order shortly before his death in 2005.

Psalm Tones

Made in the USA
Coppell, TX
16 March 2021

51834703R00085